Freedom from Sin

Freedom from Sin

by
John MacArthur, Jr.

MOODY PRESS
CHICAGO

All Scripture quotations, unless noted otherwise, are from the *New Scofield Reference Bible*, King James Version. Copyright © 1967 by Oxford University Press, Inc. Reprinted by permission.

Library of Congress Cataloging in Publication Data

MacArthur, John F.
  Freedom from sin / by John MacArthur, Jr.
    p.   cm. — (John MacArthur's Bible studies)
  ISBN 0-8024-5309-0
  1. Bible.   N.T.   Romans VI, 1-VII, 25—Criticism, interpretation, etc.   2. Justification—Biblical teaching.   I. Title.   II. Series: MacArthur, John F.   Bible studies.
  BS2665.2.M19   1987
  227'.107—dc19   87-17764
                                                                        CIP

1 2 3 4 5 6 7 Printing/LC/Year 91 90 89 88 87

Printed in the United States of America

Contents

These Bible studies are taken from messages delivered by Pastor-Teacher John MacArthur, Jr., at Grace Community Church in Panorama City, California. The recorded messages themselves may be purchased as a series or individually. Please request the current price list by writing to:

WORD OF GRACE COMMUNICATIONS
P.O. Box 4000
Panorama City, CA 91412

Or call the following toll-free number:
1-800-55-GRACE

1
Dying to Live—Part 1

Outline

Introduction
A. The Background
  1. The transgression of man
  2. The justification of man
  3. The sanctification of man
B. The Barriers
  1. The bondage of legalism
  2. The boldness of libertinism
    a) Illustrated by Rasputin
    b) Illustrated by the Corinthians
  3. The balance of liberty

Lesson
I. The Antagonist (v. 1)
  A. The Quandary (v. 1a)
    1. Acts 21:26-28
    2. Galatians 2:16, 19
    3. Jude 4
  B. The Question (v. 1b)
    1. The specifics
    2. The significance
II. The Answer (v. 2)
  A. The Strong Response (v. 2a)
  B. The Startling Reality (v. 2b)
    1. The principle in salvation
    2. The permanence in salvation
      a) Colossians 1:13
      b) 2 Corinthians 5:14-17
      c) Colossians 3:1-3

III. The Argument (vv. 3-14)
   A. The Believer's Baptism into Christ (v. 3*a*)
   B. The Believer's Death and Resurrection with Christ (vv. 3*b*-5)
      1. The believer's old life (vv. 3*b*-4*a*)
         a) Our position in Christ
         b) Our practice in Christ
      2. The believer's new life (vv. 4*b*-5)
         a) Its certainty (v. 4*b*)
         b) Its fruition (v. 5)

Introduction

A. The Background

Paul's epistle to the Romans presents three major doctrinal themes. After a basic introduction and summary of redemption in Romans 1:1-17, Paul launches into a treatise on: (1) the transgression of man (1:18–3:20), (2) the justification of man (3:21–5:21), and (3) the sanctification of man (6:1–8:39).

Paul ends his epistle by discussing how Israel fits into God's future plans (9:1–11:36), giving practical examples of sanctification (12:1–15:13) and speaking of personal matters to the church in Rome (15:14–16:27).

1. The transgression of man

   Romans 1:18–3:20 shows us how utterly sinful people are. This portion of Scripture possibly gives the most definitive explanation of how guilty, hopeless, and doomed a person is apart from God.

2. The justification of man

   In this passage Paul discusses the doctrine of salvation by grace through faith alone in Jesus Christ. In response to man's dire need, God reached down and offered him full pardon through the finished work of Jesus Christ. Paul finishes his discussion on the work of Christ by saying, "The law entered, that the offense might abound.

But where sin abounded, grace did much more abound; that as sin hath reigned unto death, even so might grace reign through righteousness unto eternal life by Jesus Christ, our Lord" (Rom. 5:20-21). The work of Christ was so complete that the grace of God more than exceeds the worst of sin.

3. The sanctification of man

Beginning in Romans 6, Paul's develops a third line of thinking: the believer's holiness. Sanctification is the inevitable result of a person's forsaking his sin and coming to God.

B. The Barriers

Paul knew his discussion of man's sinfulness would inevitably bring opposition to the gospel message. He was good at anticipating the arguments of his adversaries. He had preached the gospel enough times to know the kind of responses it generated, and he knew the gaps he needed to fill to continue his own argument effectively. That is why he began his third argument by saying, "What shall we say then? Shall we continue in sin, that grace may abound?" (6:1).

1. The bondage of legalism

Many of the antagonistic Jewish leaders had a difficult time with Paul's argument about salvation by grace. They assumed it would lead to antinomianism—a disregard for the law of God. They in effect said, "Your doctrine gives far too much liberty. If more sin generates more grace, then people would continue sinning so God could be more gracious." They assumed salvation by grace through faith alone would lead to freedom gone mad. It could lead a person to think, *If the more I sin the more grace I receive, I'm going to sin like mad so God can receive more glory by giving me more grace.*

Legalists such as the Pharisees believed you had to earn favor with God through good works. They followed all the minute elements of the law, surpassing God who wrote the law. Their bondage to the law kept them from seeing that God's saving grace could free them. We know those legalistic critics accused Paul of antinomianism because in Romans 3:8 he says, "We are slanderously reported, and . . . some affirm that we say . . . Let us do evil, that good may come."

People today echo those same criticisms. Many doubt the eternal security of believers because they believe it gives far too much liberty. They say, "If you believe in eternal security, you are really saying that once a person becomes a Christian he can sin all he wants to, and God will forgive him anyway." However, such a suggestion violates the purity of God's saving grace to control people who might otherwise abuse His grace.

2. The boldness of libertinism

Not only were critics attacking Paul on negative grounds, but some were also welcoming his arguments as a justification for their own evil life-styles. The legalists objected to Paul's arguments because they said it led to antinomianism. And the antinomians (libertines) took Paul's arguments to an extreme and abandoned all obedience to God under the guise of grace.

a) Illustrated by Rasputin

Rasputin, the evil monk who influenced the Romanov family, taught and exemplified the antinomian view of salvation through repeated experiences of sin and false repentance. He believed that the more you sin, the more God gives you grace. So the more you sin with abandon, the more you give God the opportunity to glorify Himself. Rasputin declared that if you are simply an ordinary sinner, you aren't giving God an opportunity to show His glory, so you need to be an *extraordinary* sinner!

b) Illustrated by the Corinthians

The Corinthian church lived without any of the normal restraints of holiness. They were characterized by divisions (1 Cor. 1:10-11), carnality (3:1-9), incest (5:1-8), worldliness (5:9-13), lawsuits (6:1-8), fornication (6:12-20), abuse of liberty (8:1-13; 10:23-33), demon worship (10:19-22), insubordinate women (11:2-16), abuses of the Lord's Supper and love feast (11:17-34), and abuses of spiritual gifts (12:1–14:40). Such abuses typified the libertine, who pushed the doctrine of grace to an extreme.

3. The balance of liberty

Paul, however, held to neither the extremes of legalism or libertinism. He would not abandon the correct view of grace to accommodate the legalists or restrict the libertines. True, salvation is inextricably linked with sanctification. The believer is not in bondage to the law, yet he is not free to disregard the spirit behind the law: obedience to God. That is why the apostle Paul wrote Romans in the way he did. Romans 3-5 deal with how you become saved (justification), and Romans 6-8 deal with how you live after you are saved (sanctification).

There is no need to force an external control on people who are redeemed, because they are under the constant control of the Holy Spirit. The believer functions internally—with the heart—and not externally, simply following a list of rules without intrinsic motivation.

Holiness is as much a gift of God to the believer as salvation is in His redemptive act. When someone is redeemed, that is not merely a divine transaction but a miracle of transformation. God not only says you're redeemed but also begins to *make* it true. God declares us righteous and actually begins to create Christ's righteousness in us.

It is vital for the church to understand the connection between justification and sanctification. I am convinced that for the most part the American church is an unredeemed church because there is a lack of practical holiness. The life of God must be present in the one who claims to know Christ.

I. THE ANTAGONIST (v. 1)

"What shall we say then? Shall we continue in sin, that grace may abound?"

A. The Quandary (v. 1*a*)

"What shall we say then?"

Paul referred to a hypothetical antagonist, although he no doubt dealt with many people who opposed his teaching on the gospel of God's grace. He had been accused many times of preaching an antinomian gospel.

1. Acts 21:26-28—"Paul took the men, and the next day, purifying himself with them, entered into the temple, to signify the accomplishment of the days of purification, until an offering should be offered for every one of them. And when the seven days were almost ended, the Jews who were of Asia, when they saw him in the temple, stirred up all the people, and laid hands on him, crying out, Men of Israel, help! This is the man that teacheth all men everywhere against the people, and the law, and this place; and further brought Greeks also in the temple, and hath polluted this holy place."

   After collecting an offering for the poor Jerusalem church from Gentile churches, Paul went back to Jerusalem with Gentile representatives to present the gift. He wanted to show love not only in a physical way but also in a spiritual way, so he went into the Temple with some of the Gentiles to complete a vow. He wanted to show he had not abandoned his kinship to Judaism. A riot broke out because Paul brought those men into the Temple. The Jews accused him of speaking against the law, the Temple, God, and everything else they counted to be sacred. Why? Because to them the doctrine of grace seemed to be libertine teaching. Paul wanted to communicate that simply entering the Temple doesn't make or break someone's spirituality. What makes or breaks someone's spirituality is whether or not he has received Christ.

2. Galatians 2:16, 19—Paul said, "A man is not justified by the works of the law, but by the faith of Jesus Christ, even we have believed in Jesus Christ, that we might be justified by the faith of Christ, and not by the works of the law; for by the works of the law shall no flesh be justified. . . . For I, through the law, am dead to the law, that I might live unto God."

The Judaizers—Jews who believed circumcision was essential for salvation—went into the Galatian region and found people teaching that you could enter into God's kingdom by God's grace alone. They countered that you first must be circumcised, followed by diligent obedience to the law of Moses, and only then could you come into God's kingdom. That is not unlike today. Most people believe you must follow all sorts of rules to be spiritual. They believe by enforcing particular rules they can fit people into a certain mold of spirituality.

3. Jude 4—Jude said, "There are certain men crept in unawares, who were before of old ordained to this condemnation, ungodly men, turning the grace of our God into lasciviousness; and denying the only Lord God, and our Lord Jesus Christ." These false teachers turn God's grace into a cloak for their own sinful activities.

I know a preacher who for his entire public ministry has lived in habitual sin. A major emphasis of his teaching has been the freedom that God's grace provides. It fits perfectly into what Paul describes in Romans 6:1-2. The problem of libertinism is as contemporary as the issue Paul dealt with in this chapter of Romans.

On the other hand, I have been accused by legalists of preaching about God's grace without having any other rules. Many pastors have said to me, "What are the rules for membership in your church? Do your members have to sign a list of rules before joining?" Many are shocked when I respond, "If the Lord lets them into His kingdom on the basis of faith alone, we ought to let them into our churches

13

on the same basis." As representatives of His church, we need not set standards higher than God's. Christianity has never been a list of rules imposed upon people to force them to become spiritual. God has a better plan.

B. The Question (v. 1b)

"Shall we continue in sin, that grace may abound?"

The critics of Paul contended that the doctrine of grace put a premium on sin. They said that if God justifies the ungodly (cf. Rom. 4:5), what is the point in being godly if God accepts us anyway?

1. The specifics

The Greek word translated "continue" in verse 1 is *epimenō*, which means "to abide," "to remain," or "to stay." The Greek preposition *epi* intensifies the verb it prefixes. The same Greek word is used of staying in a house or making residence there (cf. Acts 15:34). In Romans 6:1, Paul is in effect saying, "Shall we continue in a state of sin so we can see grace at work? Shall we who have been saved by grace sustain the same relationship to sin that we had before we were saved? Shall we continue abiding in the house of sin?"

2. The significance

Paul was posing a theological question: Is there any link between justification and sanctification? Can a person be saved yet continue in the same pattern of sinfulness? Can there be a divine transaction that has no impact in the believer's life? Many Christians believe that if you have asked Christ to come into your life, then regardless of how you live thereafter you can be sure you're going to heaven. But that is to say sanctification doesn't necessarily follow justification. Some people say you can be saved and have absolutely no fruit—no practical righteousness. They say that is not desirable, not God's will, not the best—but it is possible. Let's see what God's Word has to say about that point of view.

II. THE ANSWER (v. 2)

"God forbid. How shall we, that are dead to sin, live any longer in it?"

A. The Strong Response (v. 2a)

"God forbid."

The translators of the King James Version translated *mē genoito* as "God forbid" in verse 2, but the phrase is actually much more emphatic than that. It is an idiom denoting the strongest possible negative reaction in the Greek language, tantamount to outraged indignation. To put it in the words of my grandmother, "Perish the thought!" In contemporary vernacular it would be, "No way!" The *New American Standard Bible* comes close to the actual meaning by the translation, "May it never be!"

The very suggestion that a believer could continue in habitual sin is thoroughly abhorrent to Paul. He didn't begin his response to this hypothetical question with some great argument; he simply said, "No. By no means. Absolutely not!" For a person to claim to be a Christian yet continue in habitual sin is not only impermissible but impossible! The thought creates utter disgust. Donald Grey Barnhouse, commenting on this verse, wrote, "Holiness starts where justification finishes; and if holiness does not start, we have the right to suspect that justification has never started" (*Romans*, vol. 3 [Grand Rapids, Mich.: Eerdmans, 1961], 2:12).

B. The Startling Reality (v. 2b)

"How shall we, that are dead to sin, live any longer in it?"

1. The principle in salvation

The phrase "died to sin" (NASB*) is the fundamental premise of the entire argument of this chapter. The King James Version translates it "dead to sin," but that isn't

New American Standard Bible.

the most accurate translation. The apostle Paul wasn't speaking of the present state of the believer as daily dying to sin but the past act (Gk., *apothnēskō,* second aorist active) of being dead to sin. Paul's argument is that when a person receives Christ as Savior and Lord, he dies to sin, so it is therefore impossible for a Christian to remain in a constant state of sinfulness.

Paul is saying that death and life are incompatible. It is impossible to be dead and alive at the same time. So a Christian can't be living in sin when he has died to it. All who come to Christ make a break with sin, a definite act that took place in the past at the moment of salvation. If someone abides in a state of sin, he is not a believer. The apostle John said, "No one who is born of God practices sin, because he is born of God" (1 John 3:9, NASB). The person who remains in a constant state of sinfulness gives evidence that he has never left his unregenerate state.

2. The permanence in salvation

If you were to view sin as a realm, you would see that the believer no longer lives in that realm. However, that is not to say that Christians never sin. Paul's argument is simply this: believers have died to sin and no longer live in that dimension. Salvation is not simply a forensic transaction but also brings about the process of transforming the believer into Christlikeness. Christ died not only for what the believer did but also for who the believer is.

a) Colossians 1:13—Paul said Christ "delivered us from the power of darkness, and hath translated us into the kingdom of his dear Son."

b) 2 Corinthians 5:14-17—Paul said, "The love of Christ constraineth us, because we thus judge that, if one died for all, then were all dead; and that he died for all, that they who live should not henceforth live unto themselves, but unto him who died for them, and rose again. Wherefore, henceforth know we no man after the flesh; yea, though we have known Christ after the flesh, yet now henceforth know we him no more. Therefore, if any man be in Christ, he is a new creation; old things are passed away; behold, all things are become new." Paul was saying that since Christ died, and since Christians are by definition in Christ, all believers have therefore died to sin. Since Christ rose from the dead, we have too—as new creatures, dead to the sphere of sin, where we previously were enslaved.

c) Colossians 3:1-3—Paul said, "If ye, then, be risen with Christ, seek those things which are above, where Christ sitteth on the right hand of God. Set your affection on things above, not on things on the earth. For ye are dead, and your life is hidden with Christ in God."

Many people have reacted against the truths of Romans 6:1-14 because they're afraid it means that Paul is referring to the eradication of the believer's sin nature. I have been asked, "Do you believe that when you become a Christian you are instantly perfect?" Of course not. No Christian is ever totally perfect on this earth. What Paul is attempting to communicate is that because the believer died to sin, he simply cannot remain or reside in sin as he did before his conversion.

III. THE ARGUMENT (vv. 3-14)

In Romans 6:3-14 the apostle Paul explains what it means to have died to sin as if he were a lawyer in a courtroom. Paul—God's defense attorney—presents a series of logical truths that explain the believer's new state.

A. The Believer's Baptism into Christ (v. 3a)

"Know ye not that, as many of us as were baptized into Jesus Christ."

A person who believes Christians are free to sin betrays a lack of understanding of what a Christian is. A Christian is not someone who is merely declared righteous and then chooses to do as he pleases. By definition a Christian is one who has received Jesus Christ and desires to be wholly obedient to Him. Salvation isn't merely God's looking through the heavenly records, drawing a line through the entry "Sinner bound for hell" and penciling in, "Saved." Romans 6:3 declares that when a person is saved, his life is fused with Jesus Christ. As Paul said, the believer is baptized (Gk., *baptizō*, "immersed") into Christ.

1. 1 Corinthians 10:1-2—Paul said, "Brethren, I would not that ye should be ignorant, that all our fathers were under the cloud, and all passed through the sea, and were all baptized unto Moses in the cloud and in the sea." Paul was refering to the children of Israel's experience in the wilderness. "Baptized into Moses" means the children of Israel came under the authority of Moses. To be baptized into Moses was to be involved in all that God was doing in the life of Moses. Moses was the channel through which God spoke to the children of Israel. He was their anchor to God. In a deeper and more profound sense, believers are baptized into Jesus Christ.

   Paul was using *baptizō* in metaphorical terms in 1 Corinthians 10:1-2, for he was not referring to literal water baptism. He used that word the same way when referring to the believer's baptism with the Holy Spirit (1 Cor. 12:13), the Spirit's ministry of placing each believer into the Body of Christ. In Romans 6 the believer's baptism into Christ speaks of intimate, personal fellowship with Him.

2. 1 John 1:3—John said, "That which we have seen and heard declare we unto you, that ye also may have fellowship with us; and truly our fellowship [our union with Christ] is with the Father, and with his Son, Jesus Christ."

3. Matthew 28:20—Jesus said, "Lo, I am with you always." Christ was speaking of His intimate union with all believers.

4. 1 Corinthians 6:17—Paul said, "He that is joined unto the Lord is one spirit." When a person becomes a Christian, he begins an intimate union with Jesus Christ. A good illustration of the Greek word *baptizō* is when a person, place, or thing is put into a new environment,

thereby forever altering its relationship to its previous environment. The union between Christ and the believer is a profound concept we will never fully understand until we are glorified (cf. 1 Cor. 13:12).

5. Galatians 3:27—Paul said, "As many of you as have been baptized into Christ have put on Christ." Here Paul equates the putting on of Christ (cf. Rom. 13:14) with baptism into Christ. Those are simply two ways of conveying the same idea.

6. Colossians 2:11-12—Paul said that in Christ "ye are circumcised with the circumcision made without hands, in putting off the body of the sins of the flesh by the circumcision of Christ; buried with him in baptism, in which also ye are risen with him through the faith of the operation of God, who hath raised him from the dead." The believer in a sense participates in Christ's death, burial, and resurrection.

7. 1 Corinthians 6:15-17—Paul said, "Know ye not that your bodies are the members of Christ? Shall I, then, take the members of Christ, and make them the members of an harlot? God forbid. What? Know ye not that he who is joined to an harlot is one body? For two, saith he, shall be one flesh. But he that is joined unto the Lord is one spirit." Paul's argument is that if a believer joins himself to a prostitute sexually, he is joining Christ to that prostitute because he is in union with Christ.

8. Ephesians 2:5-6—Paul said, "When we were dead in sins, [God] hath made us alive together with Christ (by grace ye are saved), and hath raised us up together, and made us sit together in heavenly places in Christ Jesus." All true believers have died with Christ, are risen with Christ, have ascended with Christ, and now presently reign with Christ.

9. Revelation 3:21—Jesus said, "To him that overcometh will I grant to sit with me in my throne, even as I also overcame, and am set down with my Father in his throne."

10. 2 Peter 1:3-4—Peter said, "His divine power hath given unto us all things that pertain unto life and godliness, through the knowledge of him that hath called us to glory and virtue; by which are given unto us exceedingly great and precious promises, that by these ye might be partakers of the divine nature, having escaped the corruption that is in the world through lust." God has led the believer out of corruption and made him a partaker of His divine nature.

From these verses alone, we can conclude that because we are united with Christ, it is impossible for us to continue in the same relationship to sin that we had before we were saved. And because of Christ's eternal holiness, we too will become holy.

Does Romans 6 Refer to Water Baptism?

Many people interpret Paul's argument in Romans 6:3-10 as referring to water baptism. However, Paul is simply using the physical analogy of water baptism to teach the spiritual reality of the believer's union with Christ. Some have said, "If Paul weren't speaking about literal water baptism in this passage, he would have simply said, 'All who believe in Christ believe in His death and resurrection and are therefore united with Him.' Why does he use the word *baptized*?" The reason Paul used the symbol of water baptism is that it is the outward identification of an inward reality—faith in Jesus' death, burial, and resurrection. Paul was not advocating salvation by water baptism; that would have contradicted everything he had just said about salvation by grace and not works in Romans 3-5, which has no mention of water baptism.

Water baptism was a public symbol of faith in God. Often in Scripture you can substitute the word *faith* for the word *baptism*. The apostle Peter said baptism is a mark of salvation because it gives outward evidence of an inward faith in Christ (1 Pet. 3:21). Titus says the same thing in Titus 3:4-5: "After the kindness and love of God, our Savior, toward man appeared, not by works of righteousness which we have done, but according to his mercy he saved us, by the washing of regeneration." Paul says in Acts 22:16, "Why tarriest thou? Arise, and be baptized, and wash away thy sins, calling on the name of the Lord." Those verses are not saying a person is saved by water but that water baptism is a symbol of genuine saving faith.

The Roman believers were well aware of the symbol of baptism. When Paul says, "Know ye not?" in verse 3, he is in effect saying, "Are you ignorant of the meaning of your own baptism? Have you forgotten what your baptism symbolized?" They were unaware that water baptism symbolizes the spiritual reality of being immersed into Jesus Christ. The tragedy is that many mistake the symbol of water baptism as the means of salvation rather than the demonstration of it. To turn a symbol into the reality is to eliminate the reality, which in this case is salvation by grace through faith in Christ alone.

B. The Believer's Death and Resurrection with Christ (vv. 3b-5)

1. The believer's old life (vv. 3b-4a)

"Know ye not that [we] were baptized into his death? Therefore, we are buried with him by baptism into death."

Believers are identified with Christ not only in baptism but also in His death. The first part of verse 4 is a restatement of the last part of verse 3.

a) Our position in Christ

When a person comes to faith in Christ he is taken back symbolically to Christ's own death and dies, too. A death takes place within the believer, and what comes out of that grave is totally different from what went into it. We die to sin that we might be alive to God (v. 10). Dying to sin is where the believer's new life in Christ begins.

b) Our practice in Christ

Because a believer is a new creation in Christ, his new life-style is vastly different from his old. That is why a believer cannot habitually sin. He now lives in a different realm. Those who simply add Christ to their sinful life-styles are not saved at all. When a

21

person comes to Christ, he shares in His death and becomes a different person. Believers die in Christ to live in Christ. We have been justified that we might be sanctified. Those are inseparable realities.

Theologian Charles Hodge said, "There can be no participation in Christ's life without a participation in his death, and we cannot enjoy the benefits of his death unless we are partakers of the power of his life. We must be reconciled to God in order to be holy, and we cannot be reconciled without thereby becoming holy" (*Commentary on the Epistle to the Romans* [Grand Rapids, Mich.: Eerdmans, n.d.], p. 195).

2. The believer's new life (vv. 4*b*-5)

   a) Its certainty (v. 4*b*)

   "As Christ was raised up from the dead by the glory of the Father, even so we also should walk in newness of life."

   The apostle Paul said that as Christ died and rose from the dead, so His people also died to sin and rose to God. The glory that Paul refers to in verse 4 is the sum of all God's majesty and power in raising Christ from the dead. As God's glory was displayed in the resurrection of Christ, so also it should be displayed as believers walk in newness of life.

   Paul wasn't using the word *should* to refer to obligation but to divine accomplishment. Paul used a *hina* purpose clause in the Greek text, which means the verse should be translated, "in order that we might be raised to walk in newness of life." Paul is stating that the believer will walk in the newness of life. As Christ's resurrected life was the certain consequence of His death, so the believer's holy life is the certain consequence of His resurrection and death to sin.

   Paul used "newness" of life (Gk., *kainos*) to refer to a new quality or kind of life, not "new" in terms of chronology (Gk., *neos*). Righteousness now becomes the pattern for believers as opposed to the past,

22

which was characterized by habitual sin. Sin may manifest itself from time to time in the believer's life, but it will not characterize his new life-style.

Scripture is filled with descriptions of the believer's new life: we receive a new heart (Ezek. 36:26), a new spirit (Ezek. 18:31), a new name (Rev. 2:17), and a new song (Ps. 40:3). And we are considered a new creation (2 Cor. 5:17), a new creature (Gal. 6:15), and a new man (Eph. 4:24).

The word *walk* in verse 4 refers to daily spiritual conduct. That meaning is consistent throughout the New Testament. When a person becomes a Christian, the direction of his life changes. He begins to walk the right way. The quality of his life before Christ was evil, but the quality of his new life in Christ is righteous.

b) Its fruition (v. 5)

"If we have been planted together in the likeness of his death, we shall be also in the likeness of his resurrection."

Paul affirmed the truth of the believer's new life by using another analogy to sum up his thought. The Greek word for "planted together" is *sumphutos*, which means "to grow together." Believers grow together into the likeness of Jesus Christ, a truth reminiscent of the vine and the branches in John 15:1-8. Paul was saying that if believers are growing together in Christ, and if it is His power bearing fruit in us, we will become progressively more conformed to His image.

Bishop Handley Moule said, "We have 'received the reconciliation' that we may now walk, not away from God, as if released from a prison, but with God, as His children in His Son. Because we are justified, we are to be holy, separated from sin, separated to God; not as a mere indication that our faith is real, and that therefore we are legally safe, but because we were justified for this very purpose, that we might be holy.

23

. . . The grapes upon a vine are not merely a living token that the tree is a vine and is alive; they are the product for which the vine exists. It is a thing not to be thought of that the sinner should accept justification—and live to himself. It is a moral contradiction of the very deepest kind, and cannot be entertained without betraying an initial error in the man's whole spiritual creed" (*The Epistle to the Romans* [London: Pickering & Inglis, n.d.], pp. 160-61). Moule was saying that you cannot have justification in the believer without sanctification.

The Relationship Between Justification and Sanctification

Paul said, "By grace are ye saved through faith; and that not of yourselves, it is the gift of God—not of works, lest any man should boast. For we are his workmanship, created in Christ Jesus unto good works, which God hath before ordained that we should walk in them" (Eph. 2:8-10). A person isn't saved because of his good works; he is saved to produce good works.

In his hymn "And Can It Be That I Should Gain?" Charles Wesley wrote:

> Long my imprisoned spirit lay
> Fast bound in sin in nature's night;
> Thine eye defused a quick'ning ray,
> I woke, the dungeon flamed with light;
> My chains fell off, my heart was free;
> I rose, went forth and followed Thee.

Wesley knew that justification led to sanctification. If you have truly come to faith in Christ, you have also been set apart for holiness. The believer is a different person, so if you aren't different, you should examine yourself to see whether you're really in the faith (cf. 2 Cor. 13:5). A Christian is a brand-new creation in Christ. He has become something he never was before. Salvation is not an addition but a transformation. Becoming a Christian is not simply receiving some*thing* new; it is becoming some*one* new. The believer has died to sin because sin is no longer the abiding power in his life. Salvation is more than something God says; it is something He actually does in the life of a believer. That is where we must start to explain the relationship between the believer and sin.

24

Focusing on the Facts

1. What are the three major doctrinal themes of Paul's epistle to the Romans (see p. 8)?
2. What other areas does Paul cover in his epistle (see p. 8)?
3. True or false: Romans 1:18–3:20 gives a definitive explanation of the sinfulness of man (see p. 8).
4. The inevitable result of man's forsaking his sin and coming to God is his _____ (see p. 9).
5. List and describe those who would object to Paul's argument in Romans 6 (see pp. 9-11).
6. Explain why the church in Corinth is a good example of the libertine philosophy of grace (see pp. 10-11).
7. True or false: Salvation and sanctification are not necessarily linked; you can have one without the other (see p. 11).
8. Salvation is not merely a divine _____ but a miracle of _____ (see p. 11).
9. What is important for the church today to understand (see p. 11)?
10. Give examples from Scripture of how the apostle Paul was accused of preaching an antinomian gospel (see pp. 12-13).
11. What did Paul mean when he asked, "Shall we continue in sin, that grace may abound?" What was the theological issue behind his question (see p. 14)?
12. The phrase _____ _____ _____ is the fundamental premise of Paul's entire argument in Romans 6 (see p. 15).
13. Do believers still live in the realm of sin? Support your answer from Scripture (see p. 16).
14. Is the believer's sin nature eradicated at the point of salvation? If not, what exactly is Paul communicating in Romans 6:1-14 (see p. 17)?
15. With what great theological truth does Paul begin his argument in Romans 6? Explain his point (see pp. 17-18).
16. Does Romans 6:3-10 refer literally to water baptism? Why or why not (see pp. 18-20)?
17. What is the purpose for believers dying to sin (see p. 21)?
18. What are the inseparable realities of the believer's life in Christ (see p. 22)?
19. What was Paul referring to when he spoke of believers walking in newness of life (see pp. 22-23)?

20. True or false: Sin will manifest itself in the life of a believer and will continue to dominate his life-style after salvation (see p. 21).
21. What analogy does Paul use to describe believers' being in the likeness of Christ's resurrection (see p. 23)?
22. Becoming a Christian is not simply _____ something new, it is _____ someone new (see p. 24).

Pondering the Principles

1. The apostle Paul encountered much opposition from both the legalists and the libertines concerning the doctrine of justification by faith. Both types of people have existed throughout history. Legalists contend that the doctrines of justification by faith and eternal security give far too much liberty and therefore lead people to believe they can sin habitually without losing their salvation. However, the libertines welcome this doctrine as a justification for their own evil life-styles. Can a person be saved and continue to live an ungodly life-style? Do you claim to be saved yet live an unholy life-style? Study the following passages on unholy living and determine if they describe your life: 1 Corinthians 6:9-11, Galatians 5:19-24, and Revelation 21:8. Ask God to give you a clear answer about your own salvation.

2. The apostle Paul said that because the believer has died to sin and is resurrected with Christ, he should walk in newness of life. Are you walking in newness of life? Is it clear to everyone around you that you now walk according to the Spirit and not according to this world? Study the following verses about the Christian's walk: Galatians 5:16, Ephesians 5:2, Philippians 3:17-18, Colossians 1:10, and 1 John 1:7. Ask God to cause you to walk in this way.

2
Dying to Live—Part 2

Outline

Introduction
A. The Transformation
    1. Of John Newton
    2. Of the apostle Paul
    3. Of the Corinthian believers
B. The Truth

Review
  I. The Antagonist (v. 1)
 II. The Answer (v. 2)
III. The Argument (vv. 3-14)
    A. The Believer's Baptism into Christ (v. 3a)
    B. The Believer's Death and Resurrection with Christ (vv. 3b-5)

Lesson
    C. The Believer's Freedom from Sin (vv. 6-7)
        1. The believer's old nature is crucified (v. 6a)
            a) Ephesians 4:21-22
            b) 2 Corinthians 5:17
            c) Colossians 3:9-10
        2. The believer's sinfulness is rendered inoperative (v. 6b)
            a) The term
            b) The translation
                (1) Romans 3:3
                (2) Romans 3:31
                (3) Romans 4:14
                (4) Romans 7:2

  c) The task
   (1) 1 Corinthians 6:19-20
   (2) Romans 12:1-2
   (3) Romans 7:18, 23
   (4) Romans 6:16-18
   (5) Galatians 5:24
  3. The believer's master is no longer sin (vv. 6*c*-7)
   a) The constant fact
   b) The controlling force
    (1) 1 Peter 4:1-2
    (2) Romans 7:20
    (3) 2 Peter 1:3-4
D. The Believer's Death to Sin (vv. 8-10)
  1. The certainty (v. 8)
  2. The conqueror (v. 9)
  3. The climax (v. 10)
   a) Christ died once for sin
   b) Christ died to pay for sin
    (1) The penalty of sin
    (2) The power of sin

Conclusion

Introduction

A. The Transformation

 1. Of John Newton

Eighteenth-century Englishman John Newton ran away to sea early in life and finally settled in Africa, where he was enslaved by an African woman. He sank so low that he lived on the crumbs from her table. Young Newton ate wild yams, which he dug out of the ground at night. His clothing was reduced to a single shirt, which he periodically washed in the ocean. He finally escaped slavery and fled to other African natives, with whom he lived a debauched life.

However, God laid hold of John Newton through an African missionary. Newton became a sea captain and later a minister of Jesus Christ. He went on to write many great hymns, including "Amazing Grace." He became the pastor of a church in England, and to this day the church-yard carries an epitaph that Newton himself wrote (*Out of the Depths: An Autobiography* [Chicago: Moody, n.d.], p. 151):

> John Newton, Clerk,
> once an infidel and libertine,
> A servant of slaves in Africa,
> was, by the rich mercy of our Lord and Saviour,
> Jesus Christ,
> Preserved, restored, pardoned,
> And appointed to preach the faith
> He had long labored to destroy.

What so radically changed the life of John Newton?

2. Of the apostle Paul

Before his conversion the apostle Paul was a violent aggressor against the church. He said of himself: "[I] was before a blasphemer, and a persecutor, and injurious; but I obtained mercy" (1 Tim. 1:13). Paul also said, "I am crucified with Christ: nevertheless I live; yet not I, but Christ liveth in me; and the life which I now live in the flesh I live by the faith of the Son of God, who loved me and gave himself for me" (Gal. 2:20). Paul was saying that the old self is dead and a new self lives that is one with Christ. But the question remains: What so powerfully and dramatically changed him?

3. Of the Corinthian believers

Paul declared to the Corinthians, "Be not deceived: neither fornicators, nor idolaters, nor adulterers, nor effeminate, nor abusers of themselves with mankind, nor thieves, nor covetous, nor drunkards, nor revilers, nor extortioners, shall inherit the kingdom of God. And such were some of you; but ye are washed, but ye are sanctified" (1 Cor. 6:9-11). What was it that so dramatically changed all those people's lives?

B. The Truth

We find the answer to that question in Romans 6. The apostle Paul declares that only Jesus Christ can change a person from the inside out. The moment a person believes in the Lord Jesus Christ he is crucified and buried with Christ by a divine miracle and then raised with Him to a new life. Believers' lives are literally transformed.

The great theme Paul develops in Romans 6-8 is the inevitable sanctification of the believer. In Romans 5 Paul states that the first result of the believer's justification is security. Chapter 6 describes the second result—holiness. The Lord saves us to make us holy. Paul said to the sinful Corinthians, "Unto the church of God which is at Corinth, to them that are sanctified in Christ Jesus, called to be saints" (1 Cor. 1:2). Even the Corinthian believers with all their failures and sins were nonetheless destined to holiness.

Review

I. THE ANTAGONIST (v. 1; see pp. 12-14)

II. THE ANSWER (v. 2; see pp. 15-17)

III. THE ARGUMENT (vv. 3-14)

A. The Believer's Baptism into Christ (v. 3a; see pp. 17-21)

B. The Believer's Death and Resurrection with Christ (vv. 3b-5; see pp. 21-24)

Lesson

C. The Believer's Freedom from Sin (vv. 6-7)

"Knowing this, that our old man is crucified with him, that the body of sin might be destroyed, that henceforth we should not serve sin. For he that is dead is freed from sin."

When the apostle Paul said "knowing this" in verse 6, he was making an appeal to the common knowledge of his readers. It is sad to say that he could not make such an appeal to the church today. Many Christians simply do not understand who they are in Christ. Because of that, they too often yield to sin.

I know of a pastor who counsels premarital couples to take a shower together. He tells them not to worry about sin, saying that when we sin, it is simply a manifestation of our old nature. He believes the old nature is going to sin anyway, so there's nothing believers can do about it. But according to the apostle Paul, the believer's old nature is dead and buried. With that in mind, how can we possibly serve sin? Those who hold the view that sees a dual nature in the believer could easily attempt to excuse all kinds of sins by blaming them on the old nature.

1. The believer's old nature is crucified (v. 6a)

"Our old man is crucified with him."

The apostle Paul uses the Greek word *palaios* for "old," which refers to "things not merely old, but worn out by use" (G. Abbott-Smith, *A Manual Greek Lexicon of the New Testament* [Edinburgh: T & T Clark, 1981], p. 334). Paul is saying our old nature has been worn out by use and is therefore useless, fit only to be discarded in a scrap heap. Our old nature is what we were before salvation—depraved and damned. Paul said, "By one man [Adam] sin entered into the world, and death by sin, and so death passed upon all men, for all have sinned" (Rom. 5:12). Being in Adam was to be in sin, but being in Christ is to be in grace. First Corinthians 15:22 says, "As in Adam all die, even so in Christ shall all be made alive." The old nature, then, is the Adamic nature.

The apostle Paul said, "I am crucified with Christ: nevertheless I live; yet not I [Gk., *egō*; not my old nature], but Christ liveth in me; and the life which I now live in the flesh I live by the faith of the Son of God, who loved me and gave himself for me" (Gal. 2:20). I believe it is a serious misunderstanding to think of the believer as having both an old and new nature. Believers do not have dual personalities. Since there is no such thing as an old nature in the believer, what then is the correct meaning of the phrase "old man"?

a) Ephesians 4:21-22—Paul said, "If so be that ye have heard him, and have been taught by him, as the truth is in Jesus: that ye put off concerning the former manner of life the old man, which is corrupt according to the deceitful lusts." The apostle Paul here describes the old man as the believer's former, unregenerate self. He contrasts it in verse 24 by saying, "Ye put on the new man, which after God is created in righteousness and true holiness."

Some people assume Paul is giving a command to put off the old nature as if it were still in the believer, but Paul is simply stating the fact that the old nature is dead. He used an infinitive in the Greek text to describe the believer's putting off of the old nature. Commentator John Murray translates Ephesians 4:22 to read, "So that ye have put off according to the former manner of life the old man" (*Principles of Conduct* [Grand Rapids: Eerdmans, 1957], pp. 211-19). It is not a command but a statement of fact.

Bishop Handley Moule translated the verse, "Our old man, our old state, as out of Christ and under Adam's headship, under guilt and in moral bondage, was crucified with Christ" (*The Epistle to the Romans* [London: Pickering & Inglis, n.d.], p. 164). Commentator Martyn Lloyd-Jones translated it, "Do not go on living as if you were still that old man, because that old man has died. Do not go living as if he was still there" (*Romans: An Exposition of Chapter 6* [Grand Rapids, Mich.: Zondervan, 1972], p. 64). Even if someone insisted that verse 22 is a command, it only serves to establish the fact that since the old nature is dead, the believer is to practice that positional truth.

b) 2 Corinthians 5:17—Paul said, "If any man be in Christ, he is a new creation; old things are passed away; behold, all things are become new." I believe that the popular theological concept of the old man and new man fighting each other is not biblically accurate. According to the apostle Paul, the old man has been put off, having been replaced by the new man.

c) Colossians 3:9-10—Paul said, "Lie not one to another, seeing that ye have put off the old man with his deeds, and have put on the new man, that is renewed in knowledge after the image of him that created him." This passage provides the best possible interpretation of Ephesians 4:22 because the book of Colossians is parallel to the book of Ephesians. Paul is simply defining what a Christian is—one who has already put off the old nature.

Paul insists in Romans 6 that the doctrine of justification causes a person to completely divorce his old sin nature. That is not a process but a reality. To suppose, as some do, that the believer's old nature has been crucified but has risen from the grave is to contradict the entire point of Paul's argument. The believer's old sin nature has already been crucified; it is not in the process of being crucified. Some people constantly say, "I must crucify my old nature." If you think that way you are wasting your time, because according to Romans 6:6 the believer's old nature has already been crucified.

The believer is a new creation—not a perfected creation—but still a new creation. The old man is unregenerate, and the new man is regenerate. The believer is one new man. The old man has ceased to exist. Salvation brings about a radical change in the nature of the believer. So if someone continues to live in the same relationship to sin as he did before professing faith in Christ, he has not been redeemed, regardless of what he claims.

2. The believer's sinfulness is rendered inoperative (v. 6b)

"The body of sin might be destroyed."

a) The term

"The body of sin" is best seen as referring to sin's absolute domination over the life of the unbeliever. A person's body before salvation is totally possessed by his own sinful nature. "Body" refers not only to the physical body but to the mind as well. However, because of the believer's union with Christ, he is no longer under the control of sin.

The apostle Paul conceived of sin as being associated with the believer's body. In Romans 8 he says, "If Christ be in you, the body is dead because of sin" (v. 10). He continues, "If the Spirit of him that raised up Jesus from the dead dwell in you, he that raised up Christ from the dead shall also give life to your mortal bodies by his Spirit that dwelleth in you" (v. 11). Paul makes a connection between the believer's physical body and sin. In Romans 8:13 he says, "If ye live after the flesh, ye shall die; but if ye, through the Spirit, do mortify the deeds of the body, ye shall live." And later in verse 23 he says that we "groan within ourselves, waiting for the adoption, that is, the redemption of our body." As long as believers have a body, they will always battle with sin.

Some Bible commentators interpret the phrase "the body of sin" as representing the entire realm of sin, but I believe that Paul is simply referring to the crucifixion of the old nature and the end of sin's reign in the life of the believer. However, that is not to say the physical body is always and only evil. Our bodies obviously have the potential for good—how else could they be offered as living sacrifices (cf. Rom. 12:1-2)? Before the believer is saved, sin totally dominates and controls his being. After a person is saved, however, sin is no longer the tyrant, and the believer is no longer its slave. That is why it is foolish for a Christian to sin. Sin's tyranny has been broken.

b) The translation

The King James Version incorrectly translates the Greek word *katargeō* "destroyed," giving the impression that the believer's sin nature has been eradicated. Therefore, many have taught that the believer's sin nature is eradicated at the moment of salvation. This is known as the doctrine of perfectionism. However, *katargeō* literally means "to render inoperative or invalid." This particular Greek word occurs twenty-seven times in the New Testament and is used several times in the book of Romans.

(1) Romans 3:3—Paul said, "Shall their [Israel's] unbelief make the faithfulness of God without effect [*katargeō*]?" The phrase "without effect" could not mean destroyed because nothing could destroy the faithfulness of God.

(2) Romans 3:31—Paul said, "Do we then make void [*katargeō*] the law through faith? God forbid; yea, we establish the law." The verse cannot refer to the destruction of the law because the law is eternal.

(3) Romans 4:14—Paul said, "If they who are of the law be heirs, faith is made void, and the promise made of no effect." The same Greek word is used here and is correctly translated "made of no effect." The promise of God can never be destroyed. Likewise, the believer's sin nature loses its dominance and is rendered inoperative.

(4) Romans 7:2—Paul said, "The woman who hath an husband is bound by the law to her husband as long as he liveth; but if the husband be dead, she is loosed [*katargeō*] from the law of her husband." The verse is not saying the woman is destroyed, as Romans 6:6 translates the same Greek word; it simply means that her marriage is now of no effect. She is no longer considered married to her deceased husband.

Greek scholar Joseph Henry Thayer says *katargeō* means "to render idle, unemployed, inactive, inoperative," to deprive of its strength, to deprive of force, influence, or power, bring to nought, make of none effect" (*Greek-English Lexicon of the New Testament*

[Grand Rapids, Mich.: Zondervan, 1962], p. 336). The believer's body of sin has been deprived of its controlling power. J. B. Phillips translates Romans 6:6, "Let us never forget that our old selves died with him on the cross that the tyranny of sin over us might be broken."

c) The task

(1) 1 Corinthians 6:19-20—Paul said, "Know ye not that your body is the temple of the Holy Spirit who is in you, whom ye have of God, and ye are not your own? For ye are bought with a price; therefore, glorify God in your body." Paul said that since your body is the temple of the Holy Spirit and not under the domination of sin, you should not be involved in sexual sin.

(2) Romans 12:1-2—Paul said, "I beseech you therefore, brethren, by the mercies of God, that ye present your bodies a living sacrifice, holy, acceptable unto God, which is your reasonable service. And be not conformed to this world, but be ye transformed by the renewing of your mind, that ye may prove what is that good, and acceptable, and perfect, will of God."

(3) Romans 7:18, 23—Paul said, "I know that in me (that is, in my flesh) dwelleth no good thing. . . . I see another law in my members, warring against the law of my mind, and bringing me into captivity to the law of sin which is in my members." In both verses Paul refers to his humanness—that innate tendency to pursue evil and sin. Sinful instincts, bents, and propensities become a beachhead for the attack of Satan to lead believers into sin. The body in Paul's terminology is the vehicle by which sin manifests itself in the believer. The body is the unredeemed portion of believers, and it is here that Satan tempts believers to sin.

An unregenerate person can do no good work for God. A nonbeliever can do acts that may appear to be good, but they are not good works as far as God is concerned because all is to be done for His glory (1 Cor. 10:31). An unbeliever might do something that benefits other human beings, but it won't be of benefit to God. Only when a person becomes a Christian can the tyranny of sin be broken. Only then is he able to secure a new controlling agent—the Holy Spirit—in which to rightly glorify God.

(4) Romans 6:16-18—Paul said, "Know ye not that to whom ye yield yourselves servants to obey, his servants ye are whom ye obey, whether of sin unto death, or of obedience unto righteousness? But God be thanked, that whereas ye were the servants of sin, ye have obeyed from the heart that form of doctrine which was delivered you. Being, then, made free from sin, ye became the servants of righteousness." God is the believer's new master. Sin is no longer the controlling monarch.

(5) Galatians 5:24—Paul said, "They that are Christ's have crucified the flesh with the affections and lusts." The believer's flesh has been neutralized in terms of its dominance but not necessarily in terms of its presence. That is why the believer must control his flesh and not allow it to control him.

3. The believer's master is no longer sin (vv. 6c-7)

"We should not serve sin. For he that is dead is freed from sin."

Two Fields

Martyn Lloyd-Jones gave a good illustration of the believer and his sinful nature. In it were two fields with a road dividing them. Before he knew Christ, Lloyd-Jones lived in a field where Satan was king. Satan always told him what to do, and his humanness responded in sin. When he placed his faith in Christ, Lloyd-Jones crossed the road into a new field, which was under the dominion of Christ. Christ became the new ruler and new monarch in his life. The only problem Lloyd-Jones experienced was that sometimes he could hear Satan barking orders at him from across the road. Satan had a clever way of making him interested in his orders, even though Lloyd-Jones was no longer under Satan's dominion. Many fall prey to the very one from whom they've been delivered.

a) The constant fact

The apostle Paul wasn't saying believers won't sin, only that sin is not the dominating force in the Christian's life. The non-Christian does nothing but sin (cf. Isa. 64:6), whereas the Christian is enabled to do righteous deeds. Through our participation in the death and resurrection of Christ (Rom. 6:3-5), our old nature dies, the body of sin is rendered inoperative, and we are no longer slaves to sin. Paul said, "Ye were the servants of sin, [but] ye have obeyed from the heart that form of doctrine which was delivered you. Being, then, made free from sin, ye became the servants of righteousness" (Rom. 6:17-18).

b) The controlling force

The controlling force in the believer's life is grace, godliness, righteousness, and holiness. Paul reaffirms that in verse 7: "He that is dead is freed from sin." The believer's old nature died, rendering it powerless. That is why it is so foolish for a Christian to sin. Now the apostle Paul was not saying the believer has been freed from sin's presence. As long as the believer lives, he will continue to struggle with sinful habits and propensities. Paul's point is that in the believer's dying with Christ, sin is no longer ruling over him. If a Christian should fall into sin, however, he is not exempt from the effects of sin. The principle of cause-and-effect (Gal. 6:7-9) still applies.

(1) 1 Peter 4:1-2—Peter said, "As Christ hath suffered for us in the flesh, arm yourselves likewise with the same mind; for he that hath suffered in the flesh hath ceased from sin, that he no longer

should live the rest of his time in the flesh to the lusts of men but to the will of God." Peter was simply reiterating what Paul said. Because the believer has died with Christ, the tyranny of sin has been broken.

(2) Romans 7:20—Paul said, "If I do that I would not, it is no more I that do it, but sin that dwelleth in me." What happens when a believer sins? The new nature within him is not to blame; the sin that dwells in his body is the culprit. It is the only part of the believer that is not redeemed.

(3) 2 Peter 1:3-4—Peter said, "According as his divine power hath given unto us all things that pertain unto life and godliness, through the knowledge of him that hath called us to glory and virtue; by which are given unto us exceedingly great and precious promises, that by these ye might be partakers of the divine nature, having escaped the corruption that is in the world through lust."

The new nature of the believer is the divine nature of God planted within his life. It is the life of God in the soul of man. When the believer sins, it is the sin in the world that surrounds him and tempts him to sin. But as the believer is obedient to God on a daily basis, he will refuse to yield to that temptation. A justified person has been set free from the power of sin.

D. The Believer's Death to Sin (vv. 8-10)

"If we be dead with Christ, we believe that we shall also live with him, knowing that Christ, being raised from the dead, dieth no more; death hath no more dominion over him. For in that he died, he died unto sin once; but in that he liveth, he liveth unto God."

1. The certainty (v. 8)

"If we be dead with Christ, we believe that we shall also live with him."

The apostle Paul reiterates the same ideas he communicated in verses 3 and 5: that as believers have died with Christ, they have also risen to walk in new life with Christ. By using the future tense Paul isn't pointing to heaven; he's pointing to the believer's certainty of holiness from the moment he believes. All true believers participate in the same holy life of the Lord.

2. The conqueror (v. 9)

"Knowing that Christ, being raised from the dead, dieth no more; death hath no more dominion over him."

The certainty of the believer's new life in Christ is rooted in the fact that Christ will never have to die again. When Christ came out of the grave, He proved that He had broken the dominion of sin and death. When Christ conquered death, He also conquered sin, because sin and death are inextricably linked. Christ's resurrection was a decisive, complete, and final victory over death (cf. 1 Cor. 15:54-57).

3. The climax (v. 10)

"In that he died, he died unto sin once; but in that he liveth, he liveth unto God."

a) Christ died once for sin

That Christ died once for sin is an important theological concept in the New Testament. It is especially prominent in the book of Hebrews. Hebrews 10:10-14 says, "We are sanctified through the offering of the body of Jesus Christ once for all. And every priest standeth daily ministering and offering often the same sacrifices, which can never take away sins; but this man, after he had offered one sacrifice for sins forever, sat down on the right hand of God, from henceforth expecting till his enemies be made his footstool. For by one offering he hath perfected forever them that are sanctified." The writer makes the point many times (Heb. 7:27; 9:12, 26, 28). When Christ rose from the dead, He proved He had broken the power of sin. And since the believer identifies

40

with Christ's death and resurrection (Rom. 6:3-5), he too has permanently broken the power of sin.

b) Christ died to pay for sin

Many theologians have wrestled over Paul's phrase "[Christ] died unto sin." Some have taught that it means believers are no longer sensitive to sin, but we know from experience that's not true. The phrase specifically refers to Christ, not believers. Christ was never sensitive to sin because He could not sin (Heb. 4:15). He was never victimized by sin's dominance because He was sinless.

Others teach that the phrase is an exhortation for believers to die to sin. But that contradicts the whole of Romans 6, which states that believers have already died to sin. And it certainly could not be said of Christ that He, too, ought to die to sin. Still others say the phrase means that when Christ died to sin, He became perfect. But that can't be true because Christ was always perfect. That Christ died to sin has a double meaning.

(1) The penalty of sin

Romans 6:23 says, "The wages of sin is death." Jesus' death on the cross met sin's demand. Since believers have died with Christ, their debt has been paid. The ultimate choice for anyone is this: either pay for your own sin forever in hell or allow Christ to pay the penalty for you. The choice is yours.

(2) The power of sin

Christ not only died to abolish sin's penalty but also to break sin's power. Paul declared that God had made Christ, "who knew no sin, to be sin for us, that we might be made the righteousness of God in him" (2 Cor. 5:21). It is incomprehensible to imagine the sum total of the world's sin on Christ's shoulders, but by dying on the cross and rising from the dead, He bore that great weight of

41

sin and also broke the power of sin. He then allowed the believer to enter a new state of no longer being under the domination of sin.

Augustus Toplady must have had the two-pronged nature of Christ's death in mind when he wrote, "Be of sin the double cure, save from wrath and make me pure" ("Rock of Ages"). As the believer dies with Christ, he is saved from God's wrath. He is also made pure because he dies to the power of sin through Christ.

Conclusion

David C. Needham in *Birthright: Christian, Do You Know Who You Are?* (Portland: Multnomah, 1979) points out that a Christian is not simply a person who is forgiven, who will go to heaven, who has the Holy Spirit, or who has a new nature. A Christian has become someone he was not before. A Christian in terms of his most essential nature is a saint, a child of God, a masterpiece, and citizen of heaven. This is not only positionally true in the mind of God but also true here on earth. As mentioned in the introduction, John Newton's life was wretched before he came to Christ. But after his conversion he wrote, "I am not what I ought to be. I am not what I wish to be. I am not even what I hope to be. But by the cross of Christ, I am not what I was."

Focusing on the Facts

1. What was it that irrevocably changed the lives of John Newton, the apostle Paul, and the Corinthian believers (see pp. 27-30)?
2. True or false: There are many different organizations and religions that can transform an individual (see p. 30).
3. The great theme that Paul develops in Romans 6-8 is the inevitable _____ of the believer (see p. 30).
4. What is one of the main problems in contemporary Christianity (see p. 31)?
5. What happened to the believer's old nature (see pp. 31-33)?

6. What is the difference between being in Adam and being in Christ (see p. 31)?
7. True or false: It is a serious misunderstanding to think of the believer as having both an old and new nature (see p. 33).
8. What is the correct meaning of the phrase "old man" in Scripture? Support your answer with Bible verses (see p. 33).
9. If someone continues to live in the same relationship to sin as before professing faith in Christ, he has not been _____ (see p. 33).
10. True or false: After coming to Christ, a person can no longer sin (see pp. 34-35).
11. What is the controlling force in the believer's life (see p. 38)?
12. In what certainty is the believer's life rooted (see p. 40)?
13. What proves that Christ broke the power of sin (see p. 40)?
14. What is the double meaning in Paul's words that Christ died unto sin (see pp. 40-41)?

Pondering the Principles

1. According to Romans 6, the old nature represents a person before salvation, who exists solely in a state of habitual sinfulness. The new nature, however, describes a regenerate man who lives a life of righteousness and holiness that is honoring to God. This passage does not speak of the perfection of believers but the direction toward it. Is your life characterized by the old or new nature? Are you living in a state of habitual sinfulness, or is your life marked by a pattern of righteousness? Study the following passages from 1 John: 1:6-10, 2:15-19, and 3:9-11. If your life is characterized by unrighteousness, repent of your sins, and acknowledge Jesus Christ as your Lord and Savior.

2. Every believer has died with Christ and has therefore been freed from the penalty, power, and ultimately the presence of sin. Have you been freed from the penalty of sin? Or are you still in bondage? Would you like to break sin's power? Read the following verses in the order given: Romans 3:23, 6:23, and 10:9. Ask God to allow you the privilege of one day being separated from sin's presence.

3
Dying to Live—Part 3

Outline

Introduction
A. The Call to Holiness
B. The Call to Obedience
1. Lazarus
2. Paul

Review
I. The Antagonist (v. 1)
II. The Answer (v. 2)
III. The Argument (vv. 3-14)
A. The Believer's Baptism into Christ (v. 3*a*)
B. The Believer's Death and Resurrection with Christ (vv. 3*b*-5)
C. The Believer's Freedom from Sin (vv. 6-7)
D. The Believer's Death to Sin (vv. 8-10)

Lesson
E. The Believer's Position in Christ (v. 11*a*)
1. The foundation
a) Hosea 4:6
b) Isaiah 1:3
c) Colossians 3:8-10
2. The function
F. The Believer's Reckoning Against Sin (v. 11*b*)
1. The transaction making us dead to sin
2. The trouble believing we're dead to sin
a) Errant teaching
b) Satan's lies
c) The nonexperiential nature of salvation
d) Conflict with sin

3. The truth about being dead to sin
4. The triumph of being dead to sin
   a) Triumph over temptation
   b) Triumph over sin
   c) Triumph over death
G. The Believer's Yieldedness to God (vv. 12-14)
   1. The exhortation (v. 12a)
      a) 1 Peter 2:9-12
      b) 1 Peter 4:1-2
   2. The encumbrance (v. 12b)
      a) Romans 8:21-23
      b) Philippians 3:20-21
      c) 1 Corinthians 15:50-54
      d) Romans 7:15-20
      e) Romans 12:1
      f) 1 Corinthians 9:27
   3. The enticement (v. 12c)
   4. The effort (v. 13)
      a) The negative command
      b) The positive command
   5. The essence (v. 14)

Introduction

A. The Call to Holiness

If there is anything God wants from His children, it is their holiness. The apostle Peter said, "As obedient children, not fashioning yourselves according to the former lusts in your ignorance but, as he who hath called you is holy, so be ye holy in all manner of life, because it is written, Be ye holy; for I [God] am holy" (1 Pet. 1:14-16). The believer's holiness is basic to living out the perfect will of God.

B. The Call to Obedience

1. Lazarus

John 11:1-44 is the account of the Lord's raising Lazarus from the dead. When Jesus and the disciples came to Bethany, Lazarus had been dead for four days. When Jesus asked that the stone over his grave be removed,

46

Martha objected. She said Lazarus's body would already have started to decay. What she meant was that her brother was dead and Jesus need not bother with his body. But in spite of her protest, Jesus demanded that the grave be opened. He spoke a word, and Lazarus rose from the dead and walked out of the tomb. John 11:44 says, "He that was dead came forth, bound hand and foot with graveclothes; and his face was bound about with a cloth. Jesus saith unto them, Loose him, and let him go."

That is a marvelous account of God's resurrection power. It is also a good analogy for the Christian life. Many people who have been resurrected from their own deadness by Christ still have on their graveclothes. Like Lazarus, believers need to shed their graveclothes. They have been raised from the dead to walk in the newness of the Christian life.

2. Paul

The apostle Paul said, "That which I am doing, I do not understand; for I am not practicing what I would like to do, but I am doing the very thing I hate" (Rom. 7:15, NASB). Paul was communicating every believer's desire: to live victoriously by conquering sin. Paul also said, "I know that nothing good dwells in me, that is, in my flesh; for the wishing is present in me, but the doing of the good is not. For the good that I wish, I do not do; but I practice the very evil that I do not wish. But if I am doing the very thing I do not wish, I am no longer the one doing it, but sin which dwells in me" (vv. 18-20, NASB). There is no doubt that Paul struggled with sin, but he, like all other believers, desired the victory in Christ. Romans 6 gives the secret to victory over sin.

Review

I. THE ANTAGONIST (v. 1; see pp. 12-14)

II. THE ANSWER (v. 2; see pp. 15-17)

III. THE ARGUMENT (vv. 3-14)

A. The Believer's Baptism into Christ (v. 3a; see pp. 17-21)

B. The Believer's Death and Resurrection with Christ (vv. 3b-5; see pp. 21-24)

C. The Believer's Freedom from Sin (vv. 6-7; see pp. 30-39)

D. The Believer's Death to Sin (vv. 8-10; see pp. 39-42)

Lesson

E. The Believer's Position in Christ (v. 11a)

"Likewise."

Everything the apostle Paul discusses in Romans 6:1-10 is summarized under the word *likewise* in verse 11. It's like saying, "Things having now been settled, we move on." The reader is now to pursue the next truth.

1. The foundation

   The first ten verses of Romans 6 are doctrinal, presenting foundational truth upon which the believer can build his life. The apostle Paul uses the word *know* in verses 3, 6, and 9 to illustrate the believer's need to understand his position in Christ so that he can then live as he should. The believer's practice is always founded upon his position in Christ; duty is always founded on doctrine.

   A basic principle in the Word of God is that people must first know what is true before they can obey God.

   a) Hosea 4:6—Through the prophet Hosea God said, "My people are destroyed for lack of knowledge." The issue was not a lack of dedication, consecration, commitment, or revelation. The people didn't know; therefore they couldn't function. A person will never be able to live out what he does not know.

48

b) Isaiah 1:3—Isaiah said, "The ox knoweth his owner, and the ass, his master's crib, but Israel doth not know." The children of Israel were devoid of knowledge. They didn't know what God had done for them.

c) Colossians 3:8-10—Paul said, "Ye also put off all these: anger, wrath, malice, blasphemy, filthy communication out of your mouth. Lie not one to another, seeing that ye have put off the old man with his deeds, and have put on the new man, that is renewed in knowledge." The believer does not have to fall prey to sin's power because he knows that sin no longer has dominion over him. Sin cannot force him to do that which is against God.

2. The function

If the believer is to fully live out his new life in Christ, he must begin by knowing he is not what he used to be. Once the believer knows the foundational truths about his death, burial, and resurrection with Christ, and his victory over the penalty and power of sin, he is well on his way to victory in the Christian life. Doubts and fears become less and less because he knows he is dealing with a vanquished foe, a monarch who has been dethroned. The believer has been resurrected to new life and therefore has the confidence to strip away his graveclothes and live victoriously!

F. The Believer's Reckoning Against Sin (v. 11*b*)

"Reckon ye also yourselves to be dead indeed unto sin, but alive unto God through Jesus Christ, our Lord."

1. The transaction making us dead to sin

The second term Paul emphasizes in verse 11 is "reckon." His point is that doctrine should give way to belief. Although the believer is to understand with his mind, he also needs to move on and believe that truth in his heart. When Paul said, "Reckon ye also yourselves to be dead indeed unto sin," he was declaring that the believer is truly dead to sin. The Greek word for "reckon" is *logizōmai* and has many possible translations. It can refer to mathematical calculations (cf. Mark 15:28; Luke 22:37), but the Greek word literally means "to count," "to compute," "to calculate," "to take into account," or "to make account of."

In Romans 6:11 Paul uses *logizōmai* in a figurative sense. He did that a number of times in Romans 4, where it is translated "to impute," which means "to charge to someone's account." Paul was affirming that Christ's righteousness has been charged to the believer's account, thus declaring him righteous. In Romans 6:11 *logizōmai* refers to the believer's need to calculate and affirm the truths Paul had given in the previous ten verses. Paul was saying that the Christian needs to come to a settled confidence about the doctrinal data he had just been given.

The Christian's biography has been written in two volumes. Volume 1 is our old nature before salvation, and volume 2 is our new nature. Volume 1 ends with our death in Christ, and volume 2 begins with our resurrection in Christ. It is both impossible and inconceivable to relive volume 1 because we are dead to it.

2. The trouble believing we're dead to sin

Someone may have said to Paul, "It is hard for me to believe I no longer possesses a sin nature. It is equally hard for me to believe that I possess a new nature and that I am fit for eternity. I know that's what you're saying, but it is very difficult for me to affirm that." It is easy to see why such truths are difficult to believe.

a) Errant teaching

Many believers assume they are in bondage to sin all their lives. Many are taught that when you are saved, the Lord merely declares you saved but then leaves you in the same sinful situation you were in. It then becomes your responsibility to hack your way through the jungle of sin and its tyranny for the rest of your life. Christians are often taught that salvation is merely addition, not transformation. They therefore believe your new nature is added to your old nature, and you spend the rest of your life in a war zone.

b) Satan's lies

Satan doesn't want Christians to believe that sin's tyranny has been broken. He would much rather have Christians believe that he and his forces are in control and determine when sin gains an upper hand. Satan accuses the brethren both day and night (Rev. 12:10). He accuses them not only before God but also before other brethren. Satan will do anything he can to make Christians feel tremendously guilty about their sin. Some Christians even commit suicide because of Satan's lies and accusations. The devil does not want Christians to believe that sin is a vanquished foe.

c) The nonexperiential nature of salvation

Redemption is a divine transaction and is not experiential. It is not an emotion, although some will become emotional at the thought of being redeemed. Some who come to Christ may feel deep emotion because of past guilt or sin, while others simply accept the fact of their sinfulness and receive Christ without an outward show of emotion.

We can't experience physically what it means to die in Christ, be buried with Him in baptism, or be resurrected with Him. Redemption is a divine transaction that the believer must accept by faith. Those who are always looking for signs show little faith. They cannot accept the facts of the Word of God without seeing some external proof. Because believers can't see the reality that sin is a vanquished foe, that makes it difficult to believe. But God declares sin to be a vanquished foe, and that makes it as believable as possible.

d) Conflict with sin

The biggest difficulty in believing that sin is a vanquished foe is the constant conflict believers have with sin. When you destroy people's convenient theological categories by teaching what God really says—that there is only one nature in the believer—many don't know how to respond. David C. Needham said, "What could be more frustrating than being a Christian who thinks himself primarily to be a self-centered sinner, yet whose purpose in life is to produce God-centered holiness?" (*Birthright: Christian, Do You Know Who You Are?* [Portland: Multnomah, 1979], p. 69). It is difficult to believe we're dead to sin since we still struggle with sin, but the Christian must believe it to be true because the Bible says it is a fact. Even though Paul himself penned this liberating truth in holy Scripture, he himself struggled with his own sin (Rom. 7:15-24).

Explaining the reality that the believer has only one new nature is not simply playing a psychological word game. It isn't saying to yourself, *I'm really wonderful, holy, and righteous,* until you finally convince yourself of something that isn't true. The point is that God's Word teaches that sin's power is broken in the life of the believer, and our response is to believe that to be true.

Abraham must have had a difficult time believing God for a child because he was ninety-nine years old and his wife, Sarah, was ninety. As he looked at himself and Sarah, he must have snickered. We know that Sarah actually did laugh (cf. Gen. 18:10-15). But Romans 4:1-5 says Abraham believed God and was therefore considered righteous. He believed what God said even though it was humanly impossible.

3. The truth about being dead to sin

The doctrine of salvation by grace does not lead men to sin—that's the point Paul makes in Romans 6:1-2. It does not free up the believer to continue in sin so that God can exercise His grace. Romans 6:3-10 tells us why:

because sin's tyranny has been broken in the life of the believer. The Christian must believe that to be true. Christ's holiness is imputed to the believer, and as a result sin's dominion is made void. Christians can choose not to sin. We are never forced to sin, nor are we unfortunate victims of inherent wickedness that cannot be conquered.

Commentator Donald Grey Barnhouse said, "Years ago, in the midst of a Latin-American revolution, an American citizen was captured and sentenced to death. But an American officer rushed before the firing squad and draped a large American flag entirely around the victim. 'If you shoot this man' he cried, 'you will fire through the American flag and incur the wrath of a whole nation!' The revolutionary in charge released the prisoner at once" (*Romans,* vol. 3 [Grand Rapids, Mich.: Eerdmans, 1961], 2:118). The believer is likewise draped with the protecting righteousness of Jesus Christ, and Satan cannot shoot his bullets of accusation with lasting effect. Eighteenth-century hymn writer Isaac Watts said that in Him the tribes of Adam boast more blessings than their fathers lost. Believers are in God's eternal purpose, plan, presence, and power. We have been blessed with all spiritual blessings (Eph. 1:3). God is working out His good pleasure in us (Phil. 2:13) and will one day perfect us (Phil. 1:6).

4. The triumph of being dead to sin

What does it mean to affirm you are actually dead to sin and alive to God through Jesus Christ?

a) Triumph over temptation

Paul said, "There hath no temptation taken you but such as is common to man; but God is faithful, who will not permit you to be tempted above that ye are able, but will, with the temptation, also make the way of escape, that ye may be able to bear it" (1 Cor. 10:13). There never will be a temptation that a believer cannot have victory over. Because sin is not your lord, you can be confident when tempted by Satan.

53

b) Triumph over sin

Because the believer has been separated from the penalty of sin, he can be confident that when he does sin, he will not lose his salvation. At times, sin may rear its ugly head, and the believer may choose to obey its temptation, but that will never cause the true believer to forfeit eternal life. By its very title, eternal life is forever, and Satan can never cause a true child of God to pay the penalty for sin, because Christ paid it once and for all on his behalf. When Christ died for our sin, He died once and will never die again (Rom. 9-10). Christ's death satisfied sin's penalty and forever broke its power. Even when the believer sins, he can be confident that his redemption is secured.

c) Triumph over death

The end of sin's tyranny means the believer can have confidence in the face of death. Jesus said, "He that believeth in me, though he were dead, yet shall he live. And whosoever liveth and believeth in me shall never die" (John 11:25-26). Reckoning yourself alive to God and dead to sin allows you to face death with confident expectation.

Romans 6:11 says we are "alive to God through [lit., "in"] Jesus Christ, our Lord." Paul is again emphasizing that the believer is in an intimate union with Jesus Christ (cf. Rom. 6:3). As believers we have everything that Christ has because we are *in* Him (Eph. 1:3). Few religions claim their followers have an intimate union with their founder. You don't hear people saying, "I'm in Buddha," "I'm in Muhammed," "I'm in Confucius," "I'm in Mary Baker Eddy," "I'm in Madame Blavatsky," "I'm in Judge Rutherford," or, "I'm in Joseph Smith." But all Christians are *in* Jesus Christ.

G. The Believer's Yieldedness to God (vv. 12-14)

There are three key words the apostle Paul uses in his discussion of the believer and sin: "know" (vv. 3, 6), which has to do with the mind; "reckon" (v. 11), which has to do with the heart; and "yield" (v. 13), which has to do with the will. Paul is calling for obedience. Jesus said, "If ye know these things [His teachings], happy are ye if ye do them" (John 13:17).

1. The exhortation (v. 12*a*)

"Let not sin, therefore, reign."

Paul said that since each believer is truly dead to sin, he should not allow sin to be the dominant force in his life. Paul endeavors to show the believer in Romans 6:1-10 that sin no longer has dominion over him. Since this is a reality, the believer should not obey Satan when he barks his commands.

Paul was not saying that sin is no longer present in the believer. Sin is still a force to be dealt with. He was simply saying that sin isn't the believer's lord anymore. Paul pictures sin as a king who rules over the lives of his people, and, before people are redeemed, sin is indeed their sovereign ruler. Paul said of believers in their unregenerate state, "Ye were the servants of sin" (v. 17).

In verse 12 Paul says that since sin is not the monarch of the redeemed, we should not let it rule our lives. Since sin has no right to rule, don't allow it to. Although sin is a dethroned monarch, it is still present in the world and desires to lure the believer back into its grasp. Even though it has no right to rule, the believer sometimes allows that to happen. Thus Paul's exhortation in verse 12: "Let not sin, therefore, reign." The apostle Peter gave similar exhortations.

a) 1 Peter 2:9-12—"Ye are a chosen generation, a royal priesthood, an holy nation, a people of his own, that ye should show forth the praises of him who hath called you out of darkness into his marvelous light; who in time past were not a people but are now the people of God; who had not obtained mercy but now have obtained mercy. Dearly beloved, I beseech you as sojourners and pilgrims, abstain from fleshly lusts."

b) 1 Peter 4:1-2—"As Christ hath suffered for us in the flesh, arm yourselves likewise with the same mind; for he that hath suffered in the flesh hath ceased from sin, that he no longer should live the rest of his time in the flesh to the lust of men but to the will of God."

2. The encumbrance (v. 12*b*)

"In your mortal body."

What did Paul mean by the word *mortal*? It is a reference to the corrupted, earthly body that believers now possess, not the future glorified body believers will one day possess. Sin seeks to rule us through our physical bodies.

Before a person is saved, sin reigns not only in his body but also in his soul. Redemption renews the soul but not the body. Therefore, sin can attempt to rule only the body and not the soul. Paul does not say, "Let not sin reign in your soul," or, "Let not sin reign in your spirit." By "mortal bodies" Paul was not referring to the old sinful nature of man or even his new nature, which is the redeemed portion of believers. Man's new nature is holy, pure, and destined for heaven. What Paul meant was that the believer's physical (i.e., mortal) body is where Satan attempts to form a beachhead for sin. The dictionary defines the word *mortal* as "subject to death; having a transitory life belonging to this world." Christians, however, are new creations in Christ. Sin is still a part of the believer's flesh, but when the believer dies, he will receive a new resurrected, glorified body and will be eternally separated from the presence of sin.

a) Romans 8:21-23—Paul said, "The creation itself also shall be delivered from the bondage of corruption into the glorious liberty of the children of God. We know that the whole creation groaneth and travaileth in pain together until now. And not only they, but ourselves also, who have the first fruits of the Spirit, even we ourselves groan within ourselves, waiting for the adoption, that is, the redemption of our body." Believers are waiting for a redeemed body because the present, mortal body is susceptible to sin.

b) Philippians 3:20-21—Paul said, "Our citizenship is in heaven, from which also we look for the Savior, the Lord Jesus Christ, Who shall change our lowly body, that it might be fashioned like his glorious body." Believers are heavenly citizens, new creations (2 Cor. 5:17), partakers of God's divine nature (2 Pet. 1:4), and indwelt by the Spirit of God (Rom. 8:9). When Jesus returns, He won't change the soul, but the physical body that was once connected to a vile and sinful world will be made new.

c) 1 Corinthians 15:50-54—Paul said, "Flesh and blood cannot inherit the Kingdom of God; neither doth corruption inherit incorruption. Behold, I show you a mystery: we shall not all sleep, but we shall all be changed, in a moment, in the twinkling of an eye, at the last trump; for the trumpet shall sound, and the dead shall be raised incorruptible, and we shall be changed. For this corruptible must put on incorruption, and this mortal must put on immortality. So, when this corruptible shall have put on incorruption, and this mortal shall have put on immortality, then shall be brought to pass the saying that is written, Death is swallowed up in victory."

d) Romans 7:15-20—Paul said, "That which I do I understand not; for what I would, that do I not; but what I hate, that do I. If, then, I do that which I would not, I consent unto the law that it is good. Now, then, it is no more I that do it, but sin that dwelleth in me. For I know that in me (that is, in my flesh) dwelleth no good thing; for to will is present with me, but how to perform that which is good I find not. For the good that I would, I do not; but the evil which I would not, that I do. Now if I do that I would not, it is no more I that do it, but sin that dwelleth in me."

Paul went on to describe the believer's dilemma: "I delight in the law of God after the inward man; but I see another law in my members [bodily parts], warring against the law of my mind, and bringing me into captivity to the law of sin which is in my members. Oh, wretched man that I am! Who shall deliver me from the body of this death? I thank God through Jesus Christ, our Lord. So, then, with the mind I myself serve the law of God; but with the flesh, the law of sin" (vv. 22-25).

e) Romans 12:1—Paul said, "I beseech you therefore, brethren, by the mercies of God, that ye present your bodies a living sacrifice, holy, acceptable unto God, which is your reasonable service."

f) 1 Corinthians 9:27—Paul said, "I keep under my body [make it my slave], and bring it into subjection."

3. The enticement (v. 12c)

"That ye should obey it in its lusts."

Because of their connection with the world, our bodily lusts cry out for fulfillment. The brain and thinking processes are also a part of the body, and they demand that their lusts be obeyed. Paul says in verse 12 that sin can dominate the believer if he allows it to happen. If the believer feeds the body's lusts and entertains it with temptation, he will be dominated by it. All the sensory factors in the body that are exposed to the world's evil system can easily become channels for temptation and sin. The believer's body of sin will dominate if it is not mastered.

Key factors in living the Christian life are to obey God and deny temptation. It is invalid to say, "Let go and let God," or, "I am to do nothing, and God will do it all." Holiness is not an option for the believer; it is a command. As the believer endeavors to become more holy, God will infuse him with the ability to accomplish that task. Paul had that in mind when he said to the Philippians, "Work out your own salvation with fear and trembling. For it is God who worketh in you both to will and to do of his good pleasure" (Phil. 2:12-13). The sanctification Paul was speaking about will result only as the believer obediently pursues the perfect will of God.

Holiness in the believer's life is not an instantaneous reality but a moment-by-moment process. We must battle all our lives to be holy, because as long as we remained encased in flesh, there will be a lifetime of constant struggle. Sanctification is a process that comes to completion only when we see Jesus Christ face-to-face (cf. 1 John 3:2). When the believer is out of this body, he will then be out of this world!

4. The effort (v. 13)

   "Neither yield ye your members as instruments of unrighteousness unto sin, but yield yourselves to God, as those that are alive from the dead, and your members as instruments of righteousness unto God."

   a) The negative command

   Paul's statement, "Neither yield ye your members as instruments of unrighteousness," indicates that believers don't have to sin. It takes the expressed will of man to overcome the temptations of Satan, and that involves a choice. Our "members"—our faculties, thoughts, and reason—are not to be used for unrighteous purposes. The Greek word for "instrument" is *hoplon* and refers to a weapon, tool, or implement. It is predominately translated "weapon" in the New Testament and is the best translation for Romans 6:13 because Paul consistently used *hoplon* to communicate the word *weapon*.

   Paul sees sin as a king demanding that the believer's body be used as a weapon to promote evil. He is in effect saying, "Don't let Satan use your body to bring about unrighteousness in the world. Don't let him use you as one of his weapons."

   b) The positive command

   Implied in the word *yield* in verse 13 is the command to flee sin and pursue holiness. The believer's willingness to obey is the key factor in yielding his body as an instrument of righteousness. Paul wasn't saying there is something inherently wrong with the body. Genesis 1:31 records that before the Fall, "God saw everything that he had made, and, behold, it was very good." A believer can use his body to glorify God. Paul said, "Present your bodies a living sacrifice, holy, acceptable unto God" (Rom. 12:1). Your body is neutral; it can be used for good or evil. It can be used as a weapon for sin or as a weapon for righteousness, and the believer must decide which he will use it for.

When Paul used the phrase "as those that are alive from the dead," he was reiterating what he had said in Romans 6:1-12, specifically referring back to the word *know* in verses 3 and 6. Paul was saying, "Don't forget who you are in Christ." The believer is commanded to yield his body, which includes his mind, as a weapon of righteousness for God. And God desires to use the believer's body as a weapon of righteousness to cut through this sinful world.

5. The essence (v. 14)

"For sin shall not have dominion over you; for ye are not under the law but under grace."

Paul here climaxes the train of thought he began in verse 1 by reiterating that the tyranny of sin is broken. The believer is no longer under sin's constant control because he has died to sin and its power.

"For ye are not under the law but under grace" is a statement of our position in Christ. The believer has been relieved from the consequences of the law and is now under grace. Law and sin go together because the purpose of the law is to show man his utter sinfulness (Rom. 7:7-13). The law commands, demands, rebukes, condemns, and restrains, but it cannot conquer sin (Rom. 3:20).

To be under the law is to be damned and under the power of sin. The law of God only increases the believer's bondage by manifesting his sin and his utter inability to be righteous on his own. The law was designed to aggravate sin and as a result condemns the sinner. The law of God calls for a penalty to be paid, but the law has no ability to deliver the sinner. The grace of God embraces the believer in the righteousness of Christ.

Focusing on the Facts

1. If there is anything that God wants from His children, it is their _____ (see p. 46).
2. True or false: The believer's practice is always founded upon his position in Christ (see p. 48).
3. Describe a basic principle in the Word of God concerning the believer's knowledge. Support your answer with Scripture (see pp. 48-49).
4. When is the believer well on his way to victory in the Christian life (see p. 49)?
5. What is the believer to do after he knows he is dead to sin (Rom. 6:11; see p. 50)?
6. True or false: According to Romans 6, the believer has both an old and a new nature (see p. 50).
7. What would Satan have the Christian to believe about sin (see p. 51)?
8. Redemption is a _____ _____ that the believer must accept by faith (see p. 51).
9. Why is it difficult to believe that Christians have died to sin (see pp. 51-52)?
10. True or false: The doctrine of salvation by grace does not lead men to sin (see p. 52).
11. What three things does a believer have triumph over? Explain each (see pp. 53-54).
12. What is the significance of a believer's being in Jesus Christ (see p. 54)?
13. What are the key words the apostle Paul uses in his discussion of the believer and sin? Briefly explain each (see pp. 54-55).
14. What does Paul mean by the phrase "mortal body" (see p. 56)?
15. What will occur when believers receive a glorified, resurrected body? Use Scripture to determine your answer (see p. 56).
16. The believer's body of sin will _____ if it is not mastered (see p. 58).
17. What are key factors in living the Christian life (see p. 58)?

18. True or false: Practical holiness in the believer's life is an instantaneous reality (see p. 59).

19. What is the negative command that Paul gives for believers in Romans 6:13 (see p. 59)?

20. God desires to use the believer's body as a _____ of righteousness to _____ through this sinful world (see p. 60).

21. How does Paul bring his thoughts to a climax in Romans 6:14 (see p. 60)?

22. True or false: The law of God was designed to aggravate sin and condemn the sinner (see p. 61).

Pondering the Principles

1. A Christian must know his position in Christ before he can obey God, because obedience is built on precepts of divine truth. Are you endeavoring to act in obedience to God? Do you know your position in Christ? In many of his epistles, the apostle Paul first discussed doctrine concerning the believer and then commanded obedience based on that doctrine. He usually connected the two sections with the word *therefore*. As a long-term project, read the portions of Scripture under the doctrine category (they all precede the word *therefore*), and ask God to allow you to gain a fuller knowledge of your position in Christ:

Doctrine	Duty
Romans 1-11	Romans 12:1–16:27
Galatians 1-4	Galatians 5:1–6:18
Ephesians 1-3	Ephesians 4:1–6:24
Philippians 1-3	Philippians 4:1-23
Colossians 1:1–2:6	Colossians 2:6–4:18

2. When a Christian affirms that he is actually dead to sin and alive to God, he can have tremendous confidence over temptation, sin, and even death. Are you daily experiencing victory over those areas? Do you regularly fall to temptation and sin? When you have finished reading the above sections on doctrine, read the sections regarding your duty to God, and ask Him that you gain confidence and then victory in your battle against temptation and sin.

4
Free from Sin—Part 1

Outline

Introduction
A. The Slavery of Sin
B. The Solution to Sin

Lesson
 I. The Antagonist (v. 15*a*)
   A. The Question
   B. The Quarrel
     1. Legalists from the past
     2. Libertines from the present
 II. The Answer (v. 15*b*)
III. The Axiom (v. 16)
   A. The Assumption (v. 16*a*)
   B. The Application (v. 16*b*)
     1. The believer's true service
     2. The believer's true submission
     3. The believer's true sanctification
     4. The believer's true salvation
       a) 1 John 1:6
       b) 1 John 2:4
       c) 1 John 3:9-10
IV. The Argument (vv. 17-22)
   A. The Position (vv. 17-18)
     1. The source of salvation (v. 17*a*)
     2. The servant of sin (v. 17*b*)
     3. The standard of subjection (v. 17*c*)
       a) Titus 2:11-14
       b) 1 Peter 1:22

4. The sincerity of submission (v. 17*d*)
5. The shape of service (v. 17*e*)
6. The servant of the Savior (v. 18)

Introduction

A. The Slavery of Sin

Jesus said, "Everyone who commits sin is the slave of sin" (John 8:34, NASB). Everyone who enters the world comes under the tyranny of sin. Sin controls man's thoughts, words, and actions. The apostle Paul said the believers in Rome "were the servants [Gk., *doulos*, "bondslaves"] of sin" (Rom. 6:17, 20). Paul went on to say that the ultimate result of being a slave to sin is death (vv. 21-23).

To be a slave to sin is a horrifying thing. One man has been quoted as saying that sin "is a debt, a burden, a thief, a sickness, a leprosy, a plague, a poison, a serpent, a sting: everything that man hates it is; a load of curses, and calamities beneath whose crushing, most intolerable pressure, the whole creation groaneth. . . . Who is the hoary sexton that digs man a grave? Who is the painted temptress that steals his virtue? Who is the murderess that destroys his life? Who is this sorceress that first deceives, and then damns his soul?—Sin. Who with icy breath, blights the fair blossoms of youth? Who breaks the hearts of parents? Who brings old men's gray hairs with sorrow to the grave?— Sin.

"Who, by a more hideous metamorphosis than Ovid ever fancied, changes gentle children into vipers, tender mothers into monsters, and their fathers into worse than Herods, the murderers of their own innocents?—Sin. Who casts the apple of discord on household hearts? Who lights the torch of war, and bears it blazing over trembling lands? Who, by division in the church, rends Christ's seamless robe?—Sin. Who is this Delilah that sings the Nazirite asleep, and delivers up the strength of God into the hands of the uncircumcised? Who, winning smiles on her face, honeyed flattery on her tongue, stands in the door to offer the sacred rites of hospitality, and when suspicion sleeps, treacherously pierces our temples with a nail? What fair Siren is this, who, seated on a rock by the deadly pool, smiles to deceive, sings to lure, kisses to betray, and flings her arms around our neck, to leap with us into perdition?—Sin. Who turns the soft and gentlest heart to stone? Who hurls reason from her lofty throne, and impels sinners, mad as Gadarene swine, down the precipice, into a lake of fire?—Sin" (Dr. Guthrie, cited in Elon Foster's *New Cyclopedia of Prose Illustrations* [New York: T. Y. Crowell, 1877], p. 696).

Sin is a life-wrecking, soul-damning reality that clings to man like incurable cancer to the human breast. Men struggle to be free from sin, but they cannot. They try to flee from guilt, but no one can find relief.

B. The Solution to Sin

The greatest gift God could ever give to man is freedom from sin and right standing with Him. What a joy to fulfill all that man was intended for when God originally created him.

Romans 6:15-23 describes how to gain freedom from sin. This portion of Scripture provides tremendous comfort and is great cause for rejoicing. We place our faith in the finished work of Jesus Christ, we are "made free from sin" (vv. 18, 22). Deliverance is available to all who are haunted by their sin.

Lesson

In the book of Romans, Paul discusses the great doctrines of justification (chaps. 3-5) and sanctification (chaps. 6-8). In Romans 6:1-14 Paul unfolds the reality that believers are made holy, and in Romans 6:15-23 he describes their freedom from sin. He is approaching the same doctrine in both a positive way (holiness) and a negative way (freedom from sin). They are simply two sides of the same coin. Paul is looking at the doctrine of sanctification from two different perspectives. In verses 15-23 Paul explains that believers are sanctified because they have become slaves to God. Therefore they can no longer be slaves to sin. Paul's point in both sections of

Romans 6 is to show that a regenerated person cannot continue in the same pattern of unrighteousness that characterized his life before he was saved.

I. THE ANTAGONIST (v. 15a)

"What then? Shall we sin, because we are not under the law, but under grace?"

I have essentially used the same major outline points as in the first section of Romans 6 (see pp. 47-48) because Paul's argument in the second half follows the same pattern of thought as the first.

A. The Question

The first question of the antagonist was, "Shall we continue in sin that grace may abound?" (v. 1). The second question is much like the first: "Shall we sin, because we are not under the law, but under grace?" (v. 15). The idea in the two questions is virtually the same. Does the doctrine of salvation by grace give license to unrestrained sin? The legalist of Paul's day could not imagine that salvation is by grace through faith alone, apart from any works of the law.

B. The Quarrel

When the apostle Paul explained the doctrine of salvation by grace to the Jewish people, they rejected it because they had believed for centuries that a person must earn his way into heaven by good works. In their thinking, Paul's teaching provided liberty to sin. There have always been those who criticize the doctrine of grace because they say it leads to lawlessness. But simply because it attracts such criticism doesn't mean it should be altered to accommodate the fallen thinking of man.

1. Legalists from the past

When Paul preached the doctrine of salvation by grace through faith in the territory known as Galatia, he encountered much objection. The Jewish leaders said you must be circumcised and keep all the laws of Moses before coming to Christ. But Paul responded, "A man is not justified by the works of the Law but through faith in Christ Jesus, even we have believed in Christ Jesus, that we may be justified by faith in Christ, and not by the works of the Law; since by the works of the Law shall no flesh be justified" (Gal. 2:16, NASB). He also said to the Galatians, "I marvel that ye are so soon removed from him that called you into the grace of Christ unto another gospel, which is not another; but there are some that trouble you, and would pervert the gospel of Christ. But though we, or an angel from heaven, preach any other gospel unto you than that which we have preached unto you, let him be accursed" (Gal. 1:6-8). Salvation by grace is the true gospel. Salvation by works is an accursed gospel.

2. Libertines from the present

Many today have taken the doctrine of grace and have instead made it a doctrine of antinomianism—an attitude of lawlessness. They believe God's grace allows them to sin without consequence. I have had conversations with persons who claim to have received "super grace," thinking they don't have to confess their sin. They assume God doesn't care what they do because grace is free, and that allows them to live any way they desire. Many sins go under the name of grace. However, a person's constant state of sinfulness proves he was never under God's grace, because the grace of God inevitably transforms a life.

So, the antagonist in Romans 6:15 was asking, "Shall we deliberately, persistently, habitually sin because we are not under the law, but under grace?" That implies a complete misunderstanding of what the apostle Paul was saying. He did not mean that believers were no longer responsible to obey God's Word; his point was that we aren't under a system of law, needing to produce our own righteousness. We're to accept the free gift of God's grace. Paul's hypothetical questioner asks, "Does grace free us to sin at will?"

II. THE ANSWER (v. 15*b*)

"God forbid."

Paul's answer to the antagonist is the same as in verse 1: *me genoito*, the strongest possible negative response in the Greek language. Although the King James Version translates Paul's response as "God forbid," it would better be translated "Impossible!" "Ridiculous!" or "Absolutely not!" To the apostle Paul, the antagonist's question was an utterly unacceptable thought. To even ask a question like that would cast serious doubt on the questioner's search for truth.

III. THE AXIOM (v. 16)

A. The Assumption (v. 16*a*)

"Know ye not that to whom ye yield yourselves servants to obey, his servants ye are whom ye obey."

An axiom is a general truth that is self-evident. It doesn't need proof because it is an obvious fact. The phrase "know ye not" tells us verse 16 is an axiom. Paul is saying that if you sign up to serve a certain master, you are bound to obey that master. That is what slavery is.

B. The Application (v. 16*b*)

"Whether of sin unto death, or of obedience unto righteousness?"

Paul here personifies two masters: sin (disobedience) and obedience. Whom do men ultimately obey or disobey? God. Some people yield themselves as servants of disobedience against God, and some people yield themselves as servants of obedience to God. Slavery to sin leads to death, but slavery to obedience leads to righteousness. Theologian Charles Hodge said that men hurry "from one degrading service to another, until it wreaks their ruin" (*Commentary on the Epistle to the Romans* [Grand Rapids, Mich.: Eerdmans, n.d.], p. 206).

As Paul said earlier, men are either in Adam or in Christ (Rom. 5:12-20). They are either under the reign of sin or the reign of grace (Rom. 5:21). In Romans 6:16 Paul says that you serve either sin or obedience. There is no middle ground.

1. The believer's true service

Another axiomatic principle is that you cannot serve two masters. Jesus said, "No man can serve two masters; for either he will hate the one, and love the other; or else he will hold to the one, and despise the other" (Matt. 6:24). It is the nature of slavery that you cannot have two masters giving orders. Once you've chosen your master, you are bound to obey him.

2. The believer's true submission

Paul uses the analogy of slavery in Romans 6:15-23. He is saying that when a person becomes a Christian, he submits himself to God through Christ. There is no salvation apart from a conscious submission to Christ on the part of the believer.

Before you come to Christ, you are a slave to sin, but when you receive Christ, you become a slave to the Lord. The person who comes to God through Jesus Christ is not only ethically bound to obey but made to obey as well. Believers are "created in Christ Jesus unto good works, which God hath before ordained that we should walk in them" (Eph. 2:10).

Many people misunderstand Romans 6 because they don't realize that God brings to pass practically what He declares about believers positionally. Salvation begins with the creative act of God in totally remaking the believer's nature, and then it moves to an ethical responsibility on the part of the believer.

3. The believer's true sanctification

The apostle Paul was not giving a command in Romans 6 but was referring to the actual state of being of believers. When someone is saved, he is transformed and then is progressively sanctified. In Romans 6:1-14 Paul describes the believer's transformation through the analogy of Christ's death and resurrection, and in verses 15-23 he uses the analogy of slavery to describe the same reality.

Even though we believers are limited by our earthly bodies and can therefore experience only imperfect holiness, we will nonetheless obey because we are new creatures in Christ. Obedience is a certainty in the life of a person who is truly justified. That is not to say believers won't ever sin or that at times sin won't appear to dominate, but obedience will be manifest even if obscured at some points. Should a Christian sin, his new nature will hate that sin and yearn for righteousness as did the apostle Paul in Romans 7:15-25.

In Colossians 1:21 Paul says, "You, that were once alienated and enemies in your mind by wicked works, yet now hath he reconciled in the body of his flesh through death, to present you holy and unblamable and unreprovable in his sight." Commentator Matthew Henry said, "All the children of men are either the servants of God, or the servants of sin; these are the two families. Now, if we would know to which of these two families we belong, we must inquire to which of these two masters we yield our obedience" (*Matthew Henry's Commentary on the Whole Bible*, vol. 6 [Old Tappan, N.J.: Revell, n.d.], p. 405).

4. The believer's true salvation

The person who continues in continual and habitual sin in the same manner as before he claimed to have received Christ is not a Christian. Redemption will manifest itself in a righteous life-style. This is what the apostle John had to say about that:

a) 1 John 1:6—"If we say that we have fellowship with him, and walk in darkness, we lie, and do not the truth."

b) 1 John 2:4—"He that saith, I know him, and keepeth not his commandments, is a liar, and the truth is not in him."

c) 1 John 3:9-10—"Whosoever is born of God doth not commit sin; for his seed remaineth in him, and he cannot sin, because he is born of God. In this the children of God are manifest, and the children of the devil. Whosoever doeth not righteousness is not of God, neither he that loveth not his brother."

According to Romans 6 a believer will not continue in sin for two reasons: (1) he is united with Christ in His death, burial, and resurrection and has therefore died to the power of sin, and (2) he is the slave of God and will therefore obey Him.

IV. THE ARGUMENT (vv. 17-22)

A. The Position (vv. 17-18)

In verse 17 Paul explains the the axiom of verse 16. He then applies it to the believer's life in verses 17-22. He does so by drawing an extended contrast between slavery to sin and slavery to righteousness.

1. The source of salvation (v. 17*a*)

"God be thanked."

We owe thanks to God whenever discussing the topic of salvation because He is the source of salvation. People don't come to Christ because they are intelligent. God may appeal to the intellect in the process, but no one comes to faith in Christ for any reason other than God's sovereign will drawing him to salvation. In John 6:44 Jesus says, "No man can come to me, except the Father, who hath sent him, draw him." Paul said, "I thank my God through Jesus Christ for you all, that your faith is spoken of throughout the whole world" (Rom. 1:8). God is always to be thanked because He is the author of salvation. As you study the New Testament, you will find it emphasizes that God is the author of salvation. The transformation from death to life—from sin to God—is one that God Himself works. He alone is to be thanked for His most precious gift!

2. The servant of sin (v. 17*b*)

"Ye were the servants of sin."

The Greek tense in this phrase is imperfect, which implies the Roman believers were continually in a state of slavery to sin. Although many do not want to admit it, that is the condition of every man before salvation. Sin's dominance began with Adam and Eve and continues to this day. Every man and woman is born in slavery to sin. Paul said, "There is none righteous, no, not one: there is none that understandeth, there is none that seeketh after God. They are all gone out of the way, they are together become unprofitable; there is none that doeth good, no, not one. Their throat is an open sepulchre; with their tongues they have used deceit; the poison of asps is under their lips; whose mouth is full of cursing and bitterness. Their feet are swift to shed blood; destruction and misery are in their ways; and the way of peace have they not known. There is no fear of God before their eyes" (Rom. 3:10-18).

Unregenerate people think they are free. When confronted with the gospel of Jesus Christ, many are afraid it will restrict their liberty. But the truth is that unregenerate people don't have any liberty! There is no such thing as real freedom for an unregenerate person. All unbelievers are slaves to sin.

3. The standard of subjection (v. 17*c*)

"Ye have obeyed."

Paul has used the Greek word *hupakouete* ("obeyed") or a form of that word for the fifth time in this portion of Scripture (cf. vv. 12, 16-17). Paul is speaking about the obedience of faith. A Christian believes in Jesus Christ as an initial act of obedience and then follows through with a life of obedience. We are always to be submitting to the Master. Obedience is the expression of that faith. All who are truly justified are obedient to God, and the longer you live with Christ the more obedient you will become.

a) Titus 2:11-14—Paul said, "The grace of God that bringeth salvation hath appeared to all men, teaching us that, denying ungodliness and worldly lusts, we should live soberly, righteously, and godly, in this present age, looking for that blessed hope, and the glorious appearing of the great God and our Savior, Jesus Christ, who gave himself for us that he might redeem us from all iniquity, and purify unto himself a people of his own, zealous of good works."

b) 1 Peter 1:22—Peter said, "Ye have purified your souls in obeying the truth." When a person comes to Jesus Christ, his soul is purified. He becomes a new creation, resulting in a life of obedience.

4. The sincerity of submission (v. 17*d*)

"From the heart."

Salvation is both an external and an internal reality. It isn't something God declares on the outside without any resultant change on the inside. True salvation does not come from water baptism, church membership, religious activity, or taking a spiritual pilgrimage. Salvation comes only by faith in Christ, which results in obedience from the heart. Faith is an inward reality that produces outward obedience.

Even though salvation is the work of God, that doesn't mean a person is passively transported from slavery to sin to slavery to God. If a person becomes saved, he will know it! Some theologians say a person can be redeemed and not know it because it happened forensically, and God simply hadn't announced it yet. But in Scripture we see that salvation never occurs apart from a commitment to Christ. In Paul's words, it is obedience from the heart. Being once a slave to sin, a person who obeys Christ's call to salvation eagerly makes God his new Master.

5. The shape of service (v. 17*e*)

"That form of doctrine which was delivered you."

When someone obeys the gospel, it is not some nebulous and vague belief but a belief in the doctrine of God's good news—the body of saving truth. The way Paul framed his thinking in this verse is rich in meaning. The last part of verse 17 could better be translated, "That form of doctrine into which you were delivered," instead of, "which was delivered you."

The Greek word for "form" in verse 17 is *tupos*, which has many different uses in the New Testament. *Tupos* and its various forms are used sixteen times in the New Testament. Here it refers to a casting mold, a cast or frame into which molten material is poured to take its shape. The mold in this case is in the shape of a servant of righteousness.

When a person is born, he is poured into a mold in the shape of sin. But those who are obedient to the gospel become conformed to Christ, who is the pattern for the mold of righteousness. When God saw man as a slave to sin He melted him down in His great grace poured him into a new form or mold. Paul said to Timothy, "Hold fast the form of sound words, which thou hast heard of me, in faith and love which is in Christ Jesus" (2 Tim. 1:13).

Believers have been melted down by the convicting work of the Holy Spirit and poured into a new mold. When the metal has cooled, we are lifted out, and the new shape is that of a slave of Christ. The mold into which believers have been poured is the form of doctrine—the saving truth of the gospel of Christ. That is what Paul meant when he said, "Don't let the world around you squeeze you into its own mold, but let God remold your minds from within, so that you may prove in practice that the plan of God for you is good, meets all his demands and moves towards the goal of true maturity" (Rom. 12:2, Phillips*). The gospel teaching you submit to when you become a Christian stamps you with its image.

New Testament in Modern English.

The Stairway of Hopelessness

Christians are commanded to obey the gospel (2 Thess. 1:6-9). They must conform to the doctrine set forth in the Word of God. You cannot become a Christian by simply believing whatever you choose.

I once spoke at a luncheon for a certain businessmen's fellowship. Afterward a man said, "I've been in this group for a long time, and I'll tell you how I think you can get to God. You see, there are many steps, and at the top there is a door and behind it is this guy named Jesus. What you really want to do is try to make it up the stairs and get through the door and then hope this guy Jesus lets you in. As you're on your way up the stairs, you've got all these preachers and movements yelling at you, but you just continue going up the stairs. I call it the 'stairway of hope.' That's what I think the gospel is." I said to him, "Sir, bless your heart, you are not a Christian, and your stairway is hopeless. You need to depend on Jesus Christ alone for your salvation. You have no idea what it means to be saved."

If you expect to see Jesus some day, you cannot try to invent your own mold. There is a sound form of doctrine, the teaching of the gospel, that says you must confess your sins, believe in the Lord Jesus Christ, and affirm His death and resurrection. You must affirm His right to rule over you. That's the true gospel. If you are to come out in the image of a servant of God, you must be poured into His mold—not your own.

6. The servant of the Savior (v. 18)

"Being, then, made free from sin, ye became the servants of righteousness."

The apostle Paul was not saying that Christians are free from sinning or the temptation of sin. He was saying that those who are truly saved are free from the tyranny of sin. We are for the first time in our lives slaves of righteousness. Before a person comes to Christ he can do nothing but sin. Even unbelievers' good deeds fall into the category of sin because they're not done for the glory of God. When men do good deeds just because they want to be good men, that's tantamount to pride. Sinful men don't even know they are slaves to sin.

Believers, however, have been made free from sin and have become the servants of righteousness. Only those who believe in Jesus Christ are truly free from sin, for only Christians can choose whether to sin or not. We are free to do right for the first time in our lives. That's the essence of Christian liberty. Those who contend that our liberty in Christ gives us the freedom to sin don't understand true Christian liberty. The servant of sin has no choice but to sin, while the servant of righteousness is the only human being who has the freedom to do right for the glory of God (1 Cor. 10:31).

Focusing on the Facts

1. Everyone who enters the world comes under the _____ of _____ (see p. 64).
2. What is the ultimate result of being a slave to sin (see p. 64)?
3. True or false: The greatest gift God could ever give a human being is to be happy and successful (see p. 65).
4. In what way does the apostle Paul approach the doctrine of sanctification (see p. 65)?
5. What is Paul's point in both sections of Romans 6 (see p. 66)?
6. Why does Paul begin verses 1 and 15 with an accusation against the doctrine of salvation by grace (see p. 66)?
7. The Jewish people as a whole rejected the doctrine of salvation by grace because they believed for centuries that a person had to _____ his way into heaven by _____ (see p. 66).
8. What charge is the doctrine of God's grace always liable to (see p. 66)?
9. What problems did Paul encounter with the doctrine of grace in the territory of Galatia (see pp. 66-67)?
10. What is meant by the phrase "super grace"? What can we conclude about the salvation behind this type of thinking (see p. 67)?
11. What is Paul's answer to the antagonist's question in Romans 6:15 (see p. 68)?
12. What axiomatic principle does Paul gives in verse 16 (see p. 68)?

13. True or false: We serve either sin or obedience. There is no middle ground (see p. 69).
14. There is no salvation apart from _____ _____ to Christ on the part of the believer (see p. 69).
15. Is obedience to God an option for the believer? Explain (see p. 70).
16. What can we assume is the spiritual status of one who professes faith in Christ yet continues in habitual sin? Support your answer with Scripture (see p. 70).
17. Who is the source of our salvation? How should we respond (Rom. 6:17; see p. 71)?
18. True or false: All unregenerate people are slaves to sin and therefore have no real freedom (see p. 72).
19. A Christian believes in Jesus Christ as an initial act of _____ and then follows through with a life of _____ ____ (see p. 72).
20. What does faith produce (see p. 73)?
21. What will occur when someone obeys Christ's call to salvation (see p. 73)?
22. Explain how the Greek word *tupos* is used in Romans 6:17, and describe its significance for the believer (see p. 74).
23. True or false: You can become a Christian by believing whatever you choose (see p. 75).
24. What is the content of the gospel (see p. 75)?
25. What is Christian liberty (see p. 76)?

Pondering the Principles

1. Romans 6:16 says we will obey either sin or righteousness. Whose slave are you? Study the following texts: Joshua 24:14-27, Matthew 4:8-11, and 1 Thessalonians 1:8-9. Ask God to make you a servant of Jesus Christ.

2. Even though believers have been made righteous by God, we are not perfect. Nevertheless we are commanded to obey God on a daily basis. Are you obedient to God daily? Is the pattern of your life one of righteousness? Memorize the following verses: Matthew 5:6, 1 Timothy 6:10-12, and Hebrews 12:14. Ask God to conform you more to the image of Christ.

3. Believers have been melted down by God and poured into a new mold. We have been reshaped by the life-changing gospel of Jesus Christ. Over the course of the next week, spend time with God and ask for a fresh start. List on a piece of paper things you do that continually displease the Lord. When you are finished, look up 1 John 1:9 and write it across the page. Tear up the paper to symbolically show your break with sin. After you have destroyed the paper, study the following verses: Isaiah 64:6-8, 45:9, and Jeremiah 18:1-6. Ask God to mold you into what He desires.

5
Free from Sin—Part 2

Outline

Introduction

Review
I. The Antagonist (v. 15*a*)
II. The Answer (v. 15*b*)
III. The Axiom (v. 16)
IV. The Argument (vv. 17-22)
   A. The Position (vv. 17-18)

Lesson
   B. The Practice (v. 19)
      1. The accommodation (v. 19*a*)
         a) The form
         b) The flesh
      2. The alienation (v. 19*b*)
         a) The pollution of sin
         b) The progression of sin
      3. The affirmation (v. 19*c*)
         a) Romans 12:1
         b) 1 Corinthians 9:27
         c) 1 Thessalonians 4:3-5
   C. The Promise (vv. 20-22)
      1. Slavery to sin
         a) Delusion (v. 20)
            (1) People are sinful
            (2) People are self-righteous
         b) Deceit (v. 21*a*)
         c) Death (v. 21*b*)

Introduction

Sin is the most devastating, debilitating, and degenerating power that ever entered into the human race. Except by the intervening grace of God, it would send everyone to an eternal hell. God instructed the children of Israel to rid themselves of sin by calling it the "accursed thing" (Josh. 7:13). Sin is compared to the venom of snakes (Deut. 32:33) and the stench of death (Ps. 5:9). It is defined as a transgression of the law (1 John 3:4). Scripture characterizes sin in many ways.

A. Sin Is Defiling

    Sin is a pollution of the soul. It is to the soul what scars are to a beautiful face, what a stain is to silk, and what smog is to an azure sky. Sin makes the soul black with guilt. It is described as a menstrual cloth (Isa. 30:22), a plague (1 Kings 8:38), and filthy garments (Zech. 3:3-4). God Himself loathes false teachers who lead others to sin (Zech. 11:8). The apostle Paul calls sin "all filthiness of the flesh and spirit" (2 Cor. 7:1).

B. Sin Is Rebellious

    Sin tramples God's holy Word. It rebels against God's law and is God's would-be murderer. If sin had its way, it would eliminate or at least dethrone God.

C. Sin Is Ungrateful

Paul said that although all people have known about God, "they glorified him not as God, neither were thankful" (Rom. 1:21). Sin is like King David's son Absalom, who kissed his father yet plotted treason against him (2 Sam. 14:33–15:6). Having been the recipient of his father's goodness, treasures, and blessings, he then turned away and became a traitor. Likewise the sinner indulges in God's goodness, treasures, and blessings in the world around him; yet he too betrays God by serving Satan, who is God's archenemy. The sinner abuses God's good gifts.

D. Sin Is Incurable

Jeremiah said, "Can the Ethiopian change his skin, or the leopard his spots? Then may ye also do good, that are accustomed to do evil" (Jer. 13:23). A sinner has no more chance of changing his nature than a leopard has of changing his spots or a black person his skin. Paul said, "Unto the pure all things are pure, but unto them that are defiled and unbelieving is nothing pure; but even their mind and conscience is defiled" (Titus 1:15). Puritan John Flavel once said that all the tears of a penitent sinner, should he shed as many as have fallen drops of rain since the creation, cannot wash away sin. The everlasting burnings in hell cannot purify the flaming conscience from the least sin.

E. Sin Is Abominable

God said of sin, "Do not this abominable thing that I hate" (Jer. 44:4).

F. Sin Is Overpowering

Sin is so overpowering that it characterizes the sinner as blackness characterizes night. Sin dominates the mind, will, and affections (Jer. 44:15-17; John 3:19-21).

G. Sin Is Satanic

Paul said that sinners walk "according to the course of this world, according to the prince of the power of the air" (Eph. 2:2). Unregenerate man is a child of disobedience. Jesus said to the Jewish religious leaders, "Ye are of your father the devil, and the lusts of your father ye will do" (John 8:44).

H. Sin Is Miserable

Job said, "Man is born unto trouble, as the sparks fly upward" (Job 5:7). Paul said that "creation was made subject to vanity," which is emptiness or uselessness (Rom. 8:20). Sin takes away man's honor and peace. It ultimately takes away meaning from life.

I. Sin Is Damning

The apostle John said, "I saw the dead, small and great, stand before God, and the books were opened; and another book was opened, which is the book of life. And the dead were judged out of those things which were written in the books, according to their works. And the sea gave up the dead that were in it, and death and hades delivered up the dead that were in them; and they were judged every man according to their works. And death and hades were cast into the lake of fire. This is the second death. And whosoever was not found written in the book of life was cast into the lake of fire" (Rev. 20:12-15).

Review

B. The Practice (v. 19)

Paul has moved from speaking about the believer's position in Christ to the believer's practice in Christ. He previously stated in verse 18 that believers have become the servants of righteousness. Now in verse 19 he says we are to live righteously.

1. The accommodation (v. 19*a*)

   "I speak after the manner of men because of the infirmity of your flesh."

   a) The form

   The apostle Paul wanted his readers to realize he was using the analogy of masters and slaves to accommodate their humanness. He was attempting to communicate the eternal truths of God to the finite minds of men. In any human analogy, the logic breaks down at some points. We are to take an analogy only as far as Scripture takes it.

   b) The flesh

   The word "flesh" in verse 19 parallels the phrase "mortal body" in verse 12. They along with "body of sin" and "members" describe man's mortality, where sin finds its base of operation. It is not the new you—the new creation in Christ—that gives way to sin, but the sin that dwells in your flesh. The flesh is that part of man that is influenced by sin. As long as we are encased in fallen, fleshly bodies, we will struggle with sin.

2. The alienation (v. 19*b*)

   "Ye have yielded your members servants to uncleanness unto iniquity."

a) The pollution of sin

All unbelievers are in a state of sin and have no choice but to sin. Yielding to sin comes naturally. The Greek word translated "uncleanness" means "inward pollution," and "iniquity" means "outward lawlessness." Paul was saying that unbelievers are in the family of sin, polluted on the inside and evil on the outside. They continually yield themselves to sin both internally and externally.

b) The progression of sin

There is a progression in verse 19: first yielding the body as a servant to sin, then to uncleanness, and then to iniquity. Sin inevitably leads to more sin; it is like a cancer reproducing itself. Sin is a cruel master. Nineteenth-century British author Oscar Wilde was secretly involved in homosexual relationships as well as engaging in other deviant behavior. When his activities were discovered, he was put into prison for two years on morals charges. In his apology *De Profundis* he wrote, "I forgot that . . . what one has done in the secret chamber one has some day to shout aloud from the housetops."

Sinclair Lewis was the toast of the literary world, having received the 1930 Nobel Prize in literature. His novel *Elmer Gantry* made a mockery of Christian preachers and evangelism, the title character being a Bible-thumping, Jesus-preaching alcoholic, fornicator, and thief. However, few people know that Sinclair Lewis died as an alcoholic in a clinic outside the city of Rome (Richard O'Conner, *Sinclair Lewis* [New York: McGraw-Hill, 1971], pp. 130-35). Sin will reproduce itself until it casts a person into hell. The apostle Paul was saying that's the way the Roman believers used to be when they were under the bondage of sin.

3. The affirmation (v. 19*c*)

"Yield your members servants to righteousness, unto holiness."

In verse 19 Paul is not talking about the believer's nature. A person is either by nature a servant of sin or a servant of God (vv. 17-18). He is emphasizing that a believer's life-style must match his new nature. Believers don't have to sin. As we were once 100 percent yielded to sin, so we should now be 100 percent yielded to righteousness. Since we are freed to do right, Paul urges us to take advantage of that privilege.

a) Romans 12:1—"I beseech you therefore, brethren, by the mercies of God, that ye present your bodies a living sacrifice, holy, acceptable unto God, which is your reasonable service." Paul didn't tell believers to present their souls, but their bodies—the unredeemed part of man. He doesn't say to present your inner man because that has been transformed. The believer is to present his body because that is where the potential battleground is for sin.

b) 1 Corinthians 9:27—"I buffet [beat] my body and make it my slave" (NASB). A believer must keep his sinful body under control.

c) 1 Thessalonians 4:3-5—"This is the will of God, even your sanctification, that ye should abstain from fornication; that every one of you should know how to possess his vessel in sanctification and honor, not in the lust of sensuality, even as the Gentiles who know not God." The body has a tendency to drag believers into evil.

Being a Christian doesn't make you perfect, but you do have the capacity not to sin. Sometimes our fallen nature tempts us to sin, and we give in. But we don't have to. Not only is there a progression of evil in verse 19, but there is also a progression of righteousness. As iniquity leads to more iniquity, so righteousness leads to spiritual maturity. And the more righteous you become, the more you will gain victory over sin.

Serving a New Master

Commentator Martyn Lloyd-Jones said, "As you go on living this righteous life, and practising it with all your might and energy, and all your time . . . you will find that the process that went on before, in which you went from bad to worse and became viler and viler, is entirely reversed. You will become cleaner and cleaner, and purer and purer, and holier and holier, and more and more conformed unto the image of the Son of God" (*Romans: An Exposition of Chapter 6* [Grand Rapids, Mich.: Zondervan, 1972], pp. 268-69).

That is exactly the difference Paul describes in Romans 6:15-23 in being mastered by either the Lord or sin. Believers progress to greater and greater levels of holiness, whereas sinners regress lower and lower to the depths of depravity. No one stands still. Christians who allow themselves to sin under a deficient understanding of grace or simply give in to the flesh will find a universal principle working with believers and unbelievers alike: sin leads to more sin.

When Israel was in Egypt, God gave Pharaoh the command "Let my people go" (Ex. 7:16). But most people don't quote the rest of the verse, which says, "Let my people go, *that they may serve me*" (emphasis added). People do not correctly understand God's Word if they don't understand obedience. God didn't say, "Let My people go so they can roam around and do whatever they want the rest of their lives." God delivered the children of Israel from the bondage of their cruel masters in Egypt to become committed to a new Master. Unfortunately, it took a whole generation to learn that. We haven't been freed from sin to do only what we want but what God wants.

C. The Promise (vv. 20-22)

1. Slavery to sin

a) Delusion (v. 20)

"When ye were the servants of sin, ye were free from righteousness."

By saying that unbelievers are "free from righteousness," Paul meant that unbelievers cannot respond in righteousness to God because they do not feel the need to do so. Righteousness makes no demands on unbelievers because they have no capacity to respond righteously. That's why it does no good to tell unregenerate people to abide by God's laws.

(1) People are sinful

Unregenerate people need to recognize they are utterly incapable of keeping the law of God. That is a key point in evangelism, for only then can a person throw himself upon the mercy of Jesus Christ for salvation. There are so many who don't know Christ, yet think they are good people. However the truth is that they are slaves to sin. They assume that if they do good things, God will be satisfied. But He is pleased only when we obey Him.

(2) People are self-righteous

The apostle Paul says this about the folly of self-righteousness: "What things were gain to me, those I counted loss for Christ. Yea doubtless, and I count all things but loss for the excellency of the knowledge of Christ Jesus, my Lord; for whom I have suffered the loss of all things, and do count them but refuse [dung], that I may win Christ" (Phil. 3:7-8). A person is either a slave of sin or a slave of righteousness. There is no middle ground.

b) Deceit (v. 21a)

"What fruit had ye then in those things of which ye are now ashamed?"

Paul was asking the believer, "What fruit did you have in your unregenerate state?" The answer is none. Many without Christ boast about their unrighteous exploits, but when they come to Christ, the past is simply cause for shame.

I have noted a sense of shame in the testimonies of those with sordid backgrounds. They may want to tell how the Lord delivered them from drugs or crime, but they don't relish their sin anymore. So Paul's question in Romans 6:15 now becomes more clear. Why would someone want to come to Christ and then continue sinning when the only fruit of that sin is something to be ashamed of? John Calvin said, "As soon as the godly begin to be enlightened by the Spirit of Christ and the preaching of the gospel, they freely acknowledge that the whole of their past life, which they lived without Christ, is worthy of condemnation. So far from trying to excuse it, they are in fact ashamed of themselves. Indeed, they go farther, and continually bear their disgrace in mind, so that the shame of it may make them more truly and willingly humble before God" (*The Epistles of Paul the Apostle to the Romans and to the Thessalonians* [Grand Rapids, Mich.: Eerdmans, 1960], p. 135).

Sin does nothing but bring shame. A true believer looks back on his life before Jesus Christ and sees a lot to be ashamed of. However, people who don't know Christ tend to glory in the things believers are ashamed of.

c) Death (v. 21b)

"The end of those things is death."

Why would a Christian, who is justified by grace through faith, redeemed by Jesus Christ, and given the choice to do right, ever choose to sin? Why would someone choose to sin when sin only begets more sin, shame, and finally death? Although sin does lead to physical death, Paul is specifically referring to the second death, the death of the soul.

2. Slavery to God

a) Freedom (v. 22a)

"But now being made free from sin, and become servants to God."

It is marvelous that God doesn't hold the penalty of sin against the believer. Believers are doubly blessed because God also frees them from the tyranny of sin. Just knowing that a believer doesn't have to sin is a great reality. Paul said, "As David also describeth the blessedness of the man unto whom God imputeth righteousness apart from works, saying, Blessed are they whose iniquities are forgiven, and whose sins are covered. Blessed is the man to whom the Lord will not impute sin" (Rom. 4:6-8). Being free from sin doesn't mean you are sinless; it simply means you don't have to sin if you choose not to. Sin's capacity to control a believer is forever severed because of Christ's finished work on the cross. Believers are now slaves (Gk., *doulos*, "bondslave") of God.

b) Fruit (v. 22*b*)

"Ye have your fruit unto holiness, and the end everlasting life."

In contrast to the fruit of shame and death in verse 21, Paul now talks about the believer's fruit of holiness. He is matter-of-fact: if a person is truly saved, holiness will result. There's no such thing as a fruitless Christian. You might have to look awhile to discover the fruit of righteousness in some believers, but some measure of fruit will be evident in every true believer. Paul defines a believer's fruit as "fruit unto holiness."

Holiness is an important word because it is God's most glorious attribute. Isaiah said, "I saw also the Lord sitting upon a throne, high and lifted up, and his train filled the temple. Above it stood the seraphim: each one had six wings; with two he covered his face, and with two he covered his feet, and with two he did fly. And one cried unto another, and said, Holy, holy, holy is the Lord of hosts; the whole earth is full of his glory" (Isa. 6:1-3). Holiness is the only attribute of God that is repeated three times in a row. Although believers cannot become God, we can be like Him when we walk in holiness.

c) Fullness (v. 22*c*)

"The end everlasting life."

The fruit of unrighteousness is eternal death, but the fruit of righteousness is everlasting life. By "everlasting life" Paul wasn't just speaking about the quantity of life but also a quality of life. Living forever means nothing unless life is worth living forever. Jesus said He came that we might have abundant life (John 10:10).

V. THE ABSOLUTE (v. 23)

A. The Law of Sin (v. 23*a*)

"The wages of sin is death."

1. The inexorable law

There is a reason the sin principle in an unbeliever's life dominates him and leads him to vile behavior and ultimately to eternal death. There is also a reason that righteousness leads the believer to be holy and ultimately ushers him into the fullness of everlasting life. It's because there exists an absolute law that works without fail: "the wages of sin is death." God's inexorable law demands that the penalty for sin is eternal death. Just as the law of gravity demands that what goes up must come down, so sin demands death. Since God made inexorable laws in the physical dimension, we should not be surprised that there are inexorable laws in the spiritual dimension. Those who continue in sin earn the wages of sin, which is eternal, spiritual death.

2. The inevitable wages

The Greek word translated "wages" was commonly used of rations that were given to soldiers in military service in return for their duty. It was simply compensation for services rendered. Just as someone today would receive wages from an employer, so sinners must receive the wages of their sin—death. When God pronounces eternal hell on the unbelieving, it is because they have earned that sentence. It is just and fair because it is the proper compensation for sin. Justice demands payment. If you earn death by your sin, you will certainly receive it. Those who hope for pardon and deliverance apart from Christ are actually hoping that God will be unjust, but they are hoping for the impossible.

B. The Gift of God (v. 23*b*)

"The gift of God is eternal life through Jesus Christ, our Lord."

This is the other side to the absolute law of God. If God gives the sinner his just due, then a believer receives something he does not deserve—eternal life. Eternal life is not a wage but a gift. You cannot earn eternal life because it is a free gift. It can't be earned by good works, church attendance, philanthropy, or religious rituals. Paul said, "By grace are ye saved through faith; and that not of yourselves, it is the gift of God—not of works, lest any man should boast" (Eph. 2:8-9). If you want what you deserve—death—God will give it to you, but if you want what you do not deserve—eternal life—God will give that to you as well. How? Verse 23 tells us: "through Jesus Christ, our Lord." This is Paul's great climax to Romans 6. There is no salvation apart from the Lord Jesus Christ.

1. Acts 4:12—Peter said, "Neither is there salvation in any other; for there is no other name under heaven given among men, whereby we must be saved."

2. John 10:7-9—Jesus said, "I am the door of the sheep. All that ever came before me are thieves and robbers; but the sheep did not hear them. I am the door; by me if any man enter in, he shall be saved, and shall go in and out, and find pasture."

3. John 14:6—Jesus said, "I am the way, the truth, and the life; no man cometh unto the Father, but by me." That may be the most narrow-minded statement ever made, but it also happens to be true.

There is nothing else to say to the world other than to offer it the gift of salvation in Jesus Christ. To be made free from sin and guilt and to inherit eternal life, that is true freedom. Instead of having things to be ashamed of, a saved person is filled with thanksgiving to God. Instead of anticipating eternal death, a believer anticipates eternal life through Jesus Christ our Lord.

The Result of Grace

German theologian Dietrich Bonhoeffer said that cheap grace "amounts to the justification of sin without the justification of the repentant sinner who departs from sin and from whom sin departs. Cheap grace is not the kind of forgiveness of sin which frees us from the toils of sin. . . . Cheap grace is grace without discipleship, grace without the cross, grace without Jesus Christ. . . . [Costly grace] is the call of Jesus Christ at which the disciple leaves his nets and follows him. . . . When [Martin Luther] spoke of grace, [he] always implied as a corollary that it cost him his own life, the life which was now subjected to the absolute obedience of Christ. . . . Happy are they who, knowing that grace, can live in the world without being of it, who by following Jesus Christ, are so assured of their heavenly citizenship that they are truly free to live their lives in this world" (*The Cost of Discipleship* [New York: Macmillan, 1959], pp. 47, 53, 60).

Conclusion

Romans 6:1-14 teaches us that we are one with Christ because we have shared in His death, burial, and resurrection, and that we are to walk in newness of life. In Romans 6:15-23 we learn we have a new master. Salvation doesn't free you to sin: it frees you to do right for the first time in your life. Salvation takes unholy men and makes them holy. It is a call from sin to holiness. Any other kind of evangelism is incomplete. God is not looking for people who want to add Jesus to their sinful life-styles. Salvation is not addition; it is transformation. Jesus calls men to die to self and rise again to walk in newness of life. He is calling men who will say no to their present master and yes to a new Master. God's grace covers any sin, but it never condones it. What does it mean to be a Christian? Romans 5 says it means to be secure; chapter 6 says it means to be free from sin.

Focusing on the Facts

1. Describe what sin is and explain its effect (see pp. 80-82).
2. What is the position of every Christian, and how is he to live (see p. 83)?
3. What do the terms "flesh," "mortal body," "body of sin," and "members" refer to (see p. 83)?
4. True or false: All unbelievers are in a state of sin and have no choice but to sin (see p. 84).
5. What progression does Paul pose in Romans 6:19 (see p. 84)?
6. As we were once _____ _____ yielded to sin, so we should now be _____ _____ yielded to righteousness (see p. 85).
7. What are the two kinds of slaveries Paul speaks of in verses 20-22 (see p. 86)?
8. _____ people need to recognize they are utterly incapable of keeping the law of God (see p. 87).
9. True or false: It's not accurate to say a person is either a slave of sin or a slave of righteousness. There is a middle ground (see p. 87).
10. What is the fruit of sin? Explain (see p. 88).
11. True or false: Sin's capacity to control a believer is forever severed because of Christ's finished work on the cross (see p. 89).
12. Can a person be truly saved and exhibit no fruit throughout his life? Explain (see p. 89).
13. What does the apostle Paul mean by the phrase "everlasting life" in verse 22 (see p. 90)?
14. What is the inexorable law that Paul gives in verse 23 (see p. 90)?
15. What is the penalty for sin? Is it fair? Explain (see pp. 90-91).
16. True or false: Eternal life is not a gift but a wage (see p. 91).
17. There is nothing else to say to the world other than to offer people the gift of _____ in _____ _____ (see p. 91).
18. What do you need to clarify about salvation to keep from making your gospel presentation incomplete (see p. 92)?

Pondering the Principles

1. Sin is a devastating reality. If you fail to deal with it, it will destroy your life and send you to an eternal hell. Sin separates you

from a potential relationship with God. Read the following verses: Romans 3:23, 6:23, and 10:9-10. Confess your sinfulness to God if you haven't done so already, and ask Him to give you new life in Christ.

2. In Romans 6:21 Paul says we are all ashamed of things we did before knowing Christ. But things are different now that we are Christians. Verse 22 says we're to reproduce fruit leading to holiness. Are you producing righteous fruit? Study the following passages that speak of fruit-bearing: Proverbs 11:30, Romans 7:4, Ephesians 2:8-10, Colossians 1:10, and James 3:13-18. Ask God to produce His good work through you.

6
Dead to the Law

Outline

Introduction
A. The Glory of God's Law
  1. Psalm 19
  2. Psalm 119
B. The Importance of God's Law
  1. As seen in the Old Testament
    a) Deuteronomy 6:1-15
    b) Isaiah 42:21
    c) Psalm 138:2
    d) Exodus 18:16
    e) Malachi 4:4
  2. As seen in the Talmud
    a) Rabbi Raba
    b) Rabbi Judah
  3. As seen in Jewish thinking
    a) John 9:28-29
    b) Acts 21:20
    c) Acts 20:27-28
  4. As seen in Paul's thinking
    a) Philippians 3:4-6
    b) Acts 22:3
  5. As seen in the New Testament
C. The Inadequacy of God's Law
  1. Romans 3:19
  2. Romans 5:20

Lesson
I. The Axiom (v. 1)
A. The Basics (v. 1*a*)
B. The Brethren (v. 1*b*)

II. The Analogy (vv. 2-3)
  A. The Marriage (v. 2)
  B. The Meaning (v. 3)
    1. The binding of the law (v. 3*a*)
    2. The breaking of the law (v. 3*b*)
      a) 1 Timothy 5:14
      b) 1 Corinthians 7:39
III. The Application (vv. 4-5)
  A. The Past (v. 4*a*)
    1. The inability of the law to save
    2. The ability of God to save
  B. The Procedure (v. 4*b*)
    1. 2 Corinthians 5:21
    2. Galatians 3:13
    3. Galatians 2:19-20
  C. The Picture (v. 4*c*)
    1. Ephesians 5:24-27
    2. 2 Corinthians 11:2
  D. The Present (v. 4*d*)
  E. The Purpose (v. 4*e*)
    1. Attitude fruit
    2. Action fruit
      a) Hebrews 13:15
      b) Philippians 4:17
      c) Philippians 1:11
  F. The Problem (v. 5)
    1. Flesh (v. 5*a*)
      a) Its physical usage
        (1) 2 John 7
        (2) John 1:14
        (3) 1 John 4:2
      b) Its moral usage
        (1) Romans 8:3-10
        (2) Galatians 5:13
        (3) Ephesians 2:3
    2. Sin (v. 5*b*)
    3. Law (v. 5*c*)
    4. Death (v. 5*d*)
IV. The Affirmation (v. 6)
  A. The Deliverance (v. 6*a*)
  B. The Death (v. 6*b*)
  C. The Duty (v. 6*c*)
    1. The oldness of letter
    2. The newness of spirit

Introduction

A. The Glory of God's Law

The apostle Paul refers to the law of God twenty-three times in Romans 7. God's law is the theme of the chapter. Its intrinsic goodness needs to be established because Romans 7 speaks so much about the believer's being dead to the law. According to Scripture, the law of God is a glorious thing.

1. Psalm 19

Verses 7-10 say, "The law of the Lord is perfect, converting the soul; the testimony of the Lord is sure, making wise the simple. The statutes of the Lord are right, rejoicing the heart; the commandment of the Lord is pure, enlightening the eyes. The fear of the Lord is clean, enduring forever; the ordinances of the Lord are true and righteous altogether. More to be desired are they than gold, yea, than much fine gold; sweeter also than honey and the honeycomb." The words *law, testimony, statutes, commandments,* and *ordinances* all refer to the law of God. The psalmist is exalting God's holy law.

2. Psalm 119

The entirety of Psalm 119 is dedicated to the glory of God's law—all 176 verses! It is the longest chapter in the Bible. The psalmist said, "Blessed art thou, O Lord; teach me thy statutes" (v. 12); "I will delight myself in thy statutes" (v. 16); "Open thou mine eyes, that I may behold wondrous things out of thy law" (v. 18); "Thy law is my delight" (v. 77); "Oh, how I love thy law! It is my meditation all the day" (v. 97); "Rivers of waters run down mine eyes, because they keep not thy law" (v. 136); "Thy law is the truth" (v. 142); "Great peace have they who love thy law" (v. 165); "I have longed for thy salvation, O Lord, and thy law is my delight" (v. 174). The psalmist truly honored the law of God.

B. The Importance of God's Law

Not only is the law of God to be exalted, but it is also to be obeyed. Moses said, "Cursed be he who confirmeth not all the words of this law to do them. And all of the people shall say, Amen" (Deut. 27:26). Likewise Solomon said, "Fear God, and keep his commandments; for this is the whole duty of man" (Eccles. 12:13).

1. As seen in the Old Testament

a) Deuteronomy 6:1-15—This is the most definitive Old Testament passage conveying the character, quality, and honor of God's law. Moses commanded the children of Israel, saying, "These are the commandments, the statutes, and the ordinances, which the Lord your God commanded to teach you, that ye might do them in the land to which ye go to possess it; that thou mightest fear the Lord thy God, to keep all his statutes and his commandments which I command thee, thou, and thy son, and thy son's son, all the days of thy life; and that thy days may be prolonged. Hear therefore, O Israel, and observe to do it, that it may be well with thee, and that ye may increase mightily, as the Lord God of thy fathers hath promised thee, in the land that floweth with milk and honey.

"Hear, O Israel: The Lord our God is one Lord: and thou shalt love the Lord thy God with all thine heart, and with all thy soul, and with all thy might. And these words, which I command thee this day, shall be in thine heart; and thou shalt teach them diligently unto thy children, and shalt talk of them when thou sittest in thine house, and when thy walkest by the way, and when thou liest down, and when thou risest up. And thou shalt bind them for a sign upon thine hand, and they shall be as frontlets between thine eyes. And thou shalt write them upon the posts of thy house, and on thy gates. And it shall be, when the Lord thy God shall have brought thee into the land which he swore unto thy fathers, to Abraham, to Isaac, and to Jacob, to give thee great and goodly cities, which thou buildedst not, and houses full of all good things, which thou filledst not, and wells digged, which thou diggedst not, vineyards and olive trees, which thou plantedst not, when thou shalt have eaten and be full; then beware lest thou forget the Lord, who brought thee forth out of the land of Egypt, from the house of bondage.

"Thou shalt fear the Lord thy God, and serve him, and shalt swear by his name. Ye shall not go after other gods, of the gods of the people who are around about you (for the Lord thy God is a jealous God among you), lest the anger of the Lord thy God be kindled against thee, and destroy thee from off the face of the earth." God was saying, "Obey My commandments or be destroyed." This passage of Scripture gives high position to the revealed law of God.

b) Isaiah 42:21—The prophet Isaiah said, "The Lord is well pleased for his righteousness' sake; he will magnify the law, and make it honorable."

c) Psalm 138:2—The psalmist said, "Thou hast magnified thy word above all thy name."

d) Exodus 18:16—Moses, speaking to his father-in-law, Jethro, about his role as leader of the children of Israel, said, "I do make them know the statutes of God, and his laws."

e) Malachi 4:4—Do you know the last command in the Old Testament? The final exhortation from the prophet Malachi is, "Remember the law of Moses, my servant, which I commanded unto him in Horeb for all Israel, with the statutes and ordinances."

As you study the Old Testament, you cannot help but be overwhelmed by the dignity, character, and centrality of the law of God.

2. As seen in the Talmud

The Babylonian Talmud, the main codification of Jewish law, was completed around A.D. 500. It is inundated with the sacredness of God's law. Here are some examples:

a) Rabbi Raba

Rabbi Raba said, "The Holy One created man's evil inclination but created the Torah to overcome it" (*Baba Bathra*, 16*a*). Although that statement is an example of errant theology, it demonstrates the importance of the law to the Jewish people. They believed the law could overcome man's sinfulness.

b) Rabbi Judah

Rabbi Judah said, "The nature of the Holy One differs from that of mortal men. When a man prescribes a remedy, it may benefit one individual but injure another. But God gave the Torah [God's law] to Israel as a source of healing for all" (*Erubin*, 54*a*).

The rabbis declared that a man could make himself right with God by keeping the law. So the law was considered sacred because it was thought to be a mode of salvation.

3. As seen in Jewish thinking

By the time of the life of Christ, the Jews had elevated the law far beyond what God intended. They had made an idol out of the law, in many cases worshiping the law itself rather than the Author of the law.

a) John 9:28-29—When Jesus healed the man born blind, the Pharisees came to investigate. They reviled the blind man, saying to him, "Thou art his disciple; but we are Moses' disciples. We know that God spoke unto Moses; as for this fellow, we know not from where he is." The Pharisees were advocating the law of Moses as the only revealed truth of God, and therefore they ignored Jesus.

b) Acts 21:20—The apostle Paul had just returned to Jerusalem with Gentile believers after his missionary journeys. They brought with them gifts from Gentile churches to give to the poor Jewish believers in Jerusalem. He told the church in Jerusalem what God had done among the Gentiles, "and when they heard it, they glorified the Lord, and said to him, Thou seest, brother, how many thousands of Jews there are who believe, and they are all zealous of the law."

c) Acts 20:27-28—Paul, wanting to show his own regard for the law, went into the Temple to go through a rite of purification. Luke said, "When the seven days were almost ended, the Jews who were of Asia, when they saw him in the temple, stirred up all the people, and laid hands on him, crying out, Men of Israel, help! This is the man that teacheth all men everywhere against the people, and the law." When they grabbed Paul, a riot broke out. Had the Roman soldiers not intervened, the people would have killed him because of their zeal for God's law.

4. As seen in Paul's thinking

The testimony of the apostle Paul before his conversion echoes a similar attitude toward the law of God.

a) Philippians 3:4-6—Paul said, "Though I might also have confidence in the flesh. If any other man thinketh that he hath reasons for which he might trust in the flesh, I more: circumcised the eighth day, of the stock of Israel, of the tribe of Benjamin, an Hebrew of the Hebrews; as touching the law, a Pharisee; concerning zeal, persecuting the church; touching the righteousness which is in the law, blameless." Paul ignorantly pursued the law of God with a vengeance.

b) Acts 22:3—Paul said, "I am verily a man who is a Jew, born in Tarsus, a city in Cilicia, yet brought up in this city at the feet of Gamaliel, and taught according to the perfect manner of the law of the fathers, and was zealous toward God."

5. As seen in the New Testament

We see in the New Testament that same commitment to the sanctity, dignity, and honor of God's law.

   a) Hebrews 2:2—The writer said, "The word [the law] spoken by angels was steadfast."

   b) Acts 7:53—Stephen pointed out that the Jews "received the law by the disposition of angels."

   c) Acts 7:38—Stephen referred to the law as "the living oracles."

   d) Matthew 5:17-18—Jesus said, "Think not that I am come to destroy the law, or the prophets; I am not come to destroy, but to fulfill. For verily I say unto you, Till heaven and earth pass, one jot or one tittle shall in no way pass from the law, till all be fulfilled."

   e) Romans 7:12, 14—Paul said, "The law is holy, and the commandment holy, and just, and good. . . . The law is spiritual. . . . I delight in the law of God after the inward man."

   f) 1 Timothy 1:8—Paul said, "We know that the law is good."

   g) 1 John 3:4—The apostle John said, "Sin is the transgression of the law." The law of God brings sin to the surface.

   h) Romans 3:31—Paul said, "Do we then make void the law through faith? God forbid; yea, we establish the law." Paul, as Jesus before him, didn't want to abolish the law but to establish its rightful place.

C. The Inadequacy of God's Law

Although God's law is sacred, holy, just, and good, it is utterly incapable of producing righteousness within sinful man.

1. Romans 3:19—Paul said, "Whatever things the law saith, it saith to them who under the law, that every mouth may be stopped, and all the world may become guilty before God. Therefore, by the deeds of the law there shall no flesh be justified in his sight; for by the law is the knowledge of sin." As good as the law is, no one can be justified by trying to keep it, because doing so is impossible.

2. Romans 5:20—Paul said, "The law entered, that the offense might abound." Instead of creating righteousness, the law exposed man's extensive and utter sinfulness.

When Paul came to Christ, he seized the opportunity to defend God's grace, saying, "Sin shall not have dominion over you; for ye are not under the law but under grace" (Rom. 6:14). He explained the meaning of the phrase "sin shall not have dominion over you" in Romans 6:15-23, and he explained the meaning of the phrase "ye are not under the law but under grace" throughout Romans 7. Those who had an exalted view of the law would be devastated by his statement unless he explained what he meant. He began by explaining what it means to be free from the law.

Lesson

I. THE AXIOM (v. 1)

"Know ye not, brethren (for I speak to them that know the law), how that the law hath dominion over a man as long as he liveth?"

We will follow the same outline we have used in previous chapters. The first major outline point is an axiomatic principle Paul used to begin his defense. Paul was good at establishing self-evident, axiomatic principles that helped prove his point. An axiom isn't a profound theological statement; it's a self-evident truth that doesn't need to be proved because it's apparent. Paul's first statement in chapter 7 is patently obvious.

A. The Basics (v. 1a)

"Know ye not."

By making this statement, Paul was appealing to his audience's common knowledge. He was attempting to be tactful by giving them the benefit of the doubt. Paul was speaking to those who were well versed in the law, regardless of what law. Anyone who knows about law knows it has authority or jurisdiction only over living people.

When a drunk driver dies, you don't see a police officer writing him a ticket. The law does not apply to dead people. After President John F. Kennedy was assassinated by Lee Harvey Oswald, Oswald himself was assassinated outside the courtroom. Oswald was never tried because the law has jurisdiction only over living people. That is an obvious point.

B. The Brethren (v. 1b)

"Brethren."

Paul interjected an affectionate greeting to his critics because some of the Jewish leaders were ready to stone him on account of his comments about the law. He was tender in approaching this tension-filled subject.

II. THE ANALOGY (vv. 2-3)

A. The Marriage (v. 2)

"The woman who hath an husband is bound by the law to her husband as long as he liveth; but if the husband be dead, she is loosed from the law of her husband."

Paul's point is that a married person is bound by law to his or her spouse only as long as the spouse lives. If your spouse dies, you are no longer bound by law to him or her. The law binds people only while they are alive.

B. The Meaning (v. 3)

   1. The binding of the law (v. 3*a*)

      "If, while her husband liveth, she be married to another man, she shall be called an adulteress."

      Paul's point is that according to biblical law a person must not be married to two people at the same time. Doing so would make you an adulterer and a bigamist.

Divorce and Remarriage in Romans 7:2-3?

Paul uses the analogy of marriage in Romans 7:2-3, but he never intends to communicate a full-blown theology of marriage. Those who attempt to use Paul's analogy in this passage and expand it into a definitive statement on marriage, divorce, and remarriage are not on safe interpretative grounds.

Paul doesn't raise the issue of divorce in Romans 7:2-3. For someone to make a blanket statement—as some have—that this portion of Scripture teaches that all divorce is wrong, is to misconstrue the intent of this passage. Many have interpreted this passage to say that the only time you could ever remarry is if your partner died. They attempt to interpret Matthew 5:31-32 and Matthew 19:3-9 in light of Romans 7:2-3.

Hermeneutics—the science and art of biblical interpretation—requires that definitive passages on divorce and remarriage, such as those in Matthew 5 and 19, be used to interpret other analogous passages, instead of the reverse.

The analogy of marriage in Romans 7 is limited both in its scope and intent. Paul's point was simply to say that the law of marriage applies only as long as both partners are alive. When one dies, that law is no longer applicable to the surviving partner.

---

   2. The breaking of the law (v. 3*b*)

      "But if her husband be dead, she is free from the law, so that she is no adulteress, though she be married to another man."

A woman whose husband has died is as free as she was before she married. She is free to marry another man if she chooses.

a) 1 Timothy 5:14—Paul said, "I will, therefore, that the younger women [widows] marry, bear children, rule the house, give no occasion to the adversary to speak reproachfully."

b) 1 Corinthians 7:39—Paul said, "The wife is bound by the law as long as her husband liveth; but if her husband be dead, she is at liberty to be married to whom she will, only in the Lord."

Death permanently ends the law that binds two people in marriage. In fact, many marriage ceremonies contain the phrase "till death do us part." Unfortunately, many are eliminating that portion of their wedding vows because they do not want to be obedient to that ideal. Paul's analogy here is simple and straightforward: death ends a marriage.

III. THE APPLICATION (vv. 4-5)

"Wherefore" refers back to the axiom in verse 1. The law applies only to people that are alive.

A. The Past (v. 4a)

"Ye also are become dead to the law."

The Greek text better renders this phrase, "ye were put to death." The Greek word translated "become dead" (*ethanatōthēte*) speaks of a violent death. The same word is issued in Matthew 10:21 and Romans 8:13.

The believer was put to death at Calvary. As Paul said earlier, "Know ye not that, as many of us as were baptized into Jesus Christ were baptized into His death? Therefore, we are buried with him by baptism into death, that as Christ was raised up from the dead by the glory of the Father, even so we also should walk in newness of life. For if we have been planted together in the likeness of his death, we shall be also in the likeness of his resurrection; knowing this, that our old man is crucified with him, that the body of sin might be destroyed, that henceforth we should not serve sin. For he that is dead is freed from sin" (Rom. 6:3-7).

1. The inability of the law to save

   The law has no ability to save sinful man. Paul declared that "by the deeds of the law there shall no flesh be justified in his sight" (Rom. 3:20). All the law is capable of doing is condemning us. Earlier in our study, we learned that "the wages of sin is death" (Rom. 6:23). In Christ believers have already died, so the law cannot exact its penalty from them.

2. The ability of God to save

   Paul here used a passive verb in the Greek text (translated "are become dead") to communicate that believers don't die to the law themselves or kill themselves; they were made dead to the law in Christ through a divine act. God not only plans salvation but also carries it out. When believers die to the law it no longer has authority over them. Paul said, "There is, therefore, now no condemnation to them who are in Christ Jesus" (Rom. 8:1).

B. The Procedure (v. 4b)

"By the body of Christ."

By dying on the cross, the Lord paid sin's penalty in full and allowed man to become free from the law's demand.

1. 2 Corinthians 5:21—Paul said, "The Father hath made him [the Son] who knew no sin, to be sin for us, that we might be made the righteousness of God in him." Jesus redeemed believers from the law by His death on the cross.

2. Galatians 3:13—Paul said, "Christ hath redeemed us from the curse for the law, being made a curse for us; for it is written, Cursed is everyone that hangeth on a tree."

107

3. Galatians 2:19-20—Paul said, "I, through the law, am dead to the law, that I might live unto God. I am crucified with Christ: nevertheless I live; yet not I, but Christ liveth in me; and the life which I now live in the flesh I live by the faith of the Son of God, who loved me and gave himself for me." Believers have died to the law and come alive in Christ.

C. The Picture (v. 4c)

"That ye should be married to another."

The believer is no longer married to the law but is now married to Jesus Christ. This is a beautiful picture of the believer's relationship to Christ as His bride.

1. Ephesians 5:24-27—Paul said, "As the church is subject unto Christ, so let the wives be to their own husbands in everything. Husbands, love your wives, even as Christ also loved the church, and gave himself for it, that he might sanctify and cleanse it with the washing of water by the word; that he might present it to himself a glorious church, not having spot, or wrinkle, or any such thing; but that it should be holy and without blemish."

2. 2 Corinthians 11:2—Paul said, "I am jealous over you with godly jealousy; for I have espoused you to one husband that I may present you as a chaste virgin to Christ."

D. The Present (v. 4d)

"To him who is raised from the dead."

Paul is emphasizing Christ's present union with all believers. Christians are identified not only with Christ's death in the past, but also with a living Savior in the present. That assures the believer of his salvation. In Romans 6:9 Paul declares that Christ's death was sufficient and that He will never have to die again. Our marriage bond with Christ will last forever. The underlying point of the book of Romans is that salvation brings about a total transformation. Paul teaches us about the security of the believer (chaps. 5, 8), sanctification (chap. 6), and liberty from the law (chap. 7). Believers are free from attempting to earn their salvation. The resurrection of Jesus Christ is the key to that reality.

E. The Purpose (v. 4e)

"That we should bring forth fruit unto God."

The purpose of any believer's life is to glorify God by bearing fruit. This is not a command but a statement of fact. Paul's words could literally read, "We do bring forth fruit unto God." There is no such thing as a Christian who does not bear fruit. Salvation has a product, and that product is a transformed life that bears fruit for God. Therefore, salvation by grace through faith does anything but lead to sin! Romans 6 declares that if you know Christ, you will be holy. Romans 7 says that if you are truly married to Jesus Christ, you will bring forth fruit unto God.

Charles Hodge said, "As far as we are concerned, redemption is in order to [produce] holiness. We are delivered from the law, that we may be united to Christ; and we are united to Christ, that we may bring forth fruit unto God. . . . The only evidence of union with Christ is bringing forth fruit unto God. . . . As deliverance from the penalty of the law is in order to [produce] holiness, it is vain to expect that deliverance, except with a view to the end for which it is granted" (*Commentary on the Epistle to the Romans* [Grand Rapids, Mich.: Eerdmans, n.d.], p. 220). What kind of fruit does the apostle Paul have in mind?

1. Attitude fruit

   In Galatians 5:22-23 Paul says, "The fruit of the Spirit is love, joy, peace, long-suffering, gentleness, goodness, faith, meekness, self-control." Those are attitudes.

2. Action fruit

   a) Hebrews 13:15—The writer said, "Let us offer the sacrifice of praise to God continually, that is, the fruit of our lips giving thanks to his name."

b) Philippians 4:17—Paul said, "I desire fruit that may abound to your account."

c) Philippians 1:11—Paul prayed that the Philippians would be "filled with the fruits of righteousness, which are by Jesus Christ, unto the glory and praise of God."

Any righteous act that glorifies God is considered fruit unto Him. Christ does not transform a life simply on the basis of a historical event. He continues the transforming process because He is actively living and producing in us fruit for His own glory. Jesus said, "I am the true vine, and my Father is the vinedresser. Every branch in me that beareth not fruit he taketh away; and every branch that beareth fruit, he purgeth it, that it may bring forth more fruit" (John 15:1).

Salvation by grace doesn't give us license to sin. You do not possess true salvation if you think you will be forgiven regardless of how you live your life. The product of true salvation is holiness—the fruit that glorifies God.

F. The Problem (v. 5)

"When we were in the flesh, the sinful impulses which were by the law, did work in our members to bring forth fruit unto death."

The apostle Paul introduces four key thoughts in verse 5 that describe man's unregenerate state: flesh, sin, law, and death—a pathetic quartet. All these things operate within the same sphere. The flesh produces sin, which is stimulated by the law, resulting in death. Those four terms are a sad description of man's unregenerate state.

1. Flesh (v. 5*a*)

"We were in the flesh."

"In the flesh" means that man's sinfulness reaches the very core of his being. The word *flesh* is used two ways in the Bible.

110

a) Its physical usage

The word *flesh,* when used in its physical sense, carries with it no evil connotation.

(1) 2 John 7—John said, "Many deceivers are entered into the world, who confess not that Jesus Christ cometh in the flesh."

(2) John 1:14—John said, "The Word was made flesh."

(3) 1 John 4:2—John said, "Every spirit that confesseth that Jesus Christ is come in the flesh is of God."

b) Its moral usage

When the word *flesh* is used in its ethical or moral sense, it always has an evil connotation.

(1) Romans 8:3-10—Paul said that Christ "condemned sin in the flesh, that the righteousness of the law might be fulfilled in us, who walk not after the flesh, but after the Spirit. For they that are after the flesh do mind the things of the flesh; but they that are after the Spirit, the things of the Spirit. For to be carnally minded is death, but to be spiritually minded is life and peace. Because the carnal mind is enmity against God; for it is not subject to the law of God, neither, indeed, can be. So, then, they that are in the flesh cannot please God. But ye are not in the flesh but in the Spirit, if so be that the Spirit of God dwell in you. Now if any man have not the Spirit of Christ, he is none of his. And if Christ be in you, the body is dead because of sin, but the Spirit is life because of righteousness." Unregenerate people are of the flesh, but believers are of the Spirit.

(2) Galatians 5:13—Paul said, "Brethren, ye have been called unto liberty; only use not liberty for an occasion to the flesh" (cf. vv. 17, 19, 24).

(3) Ephesians 2:3—Paul said, "We all had our manner of life in times past in the lusts of our flesh, fulfilling the desires of the flesh."

In its ethical and moral sense, Scripture always speaks of the flesh as the believer's unredeemed body. Before we came to Christ we were engulfed in and captive to the flesh. Fortunately for the believer, however, that is history. Believers are not in the flesh.

But why is it that we continue to sin? The answer is that believers are not in the flesh, but the flesh is still in them! Although the flesh no longer makes you its slave, you still possess an unredeemed body, which remains susceptible to sin. That is why the apostle Paul said, "The whole creation groaneth and travaileth in pain together until now. And not only they, but ourselves also, who have the first fruits of the Spirit, even we ourselves groan within ourselves, waiting for the adoption, that is, the redemption of our body" (Rom. 8:22-23).

Believers, however, do not have to yield themselves to sin (Gal. 5:16). A Christian may do fleshly things because the flesh is in him, but he is not a slave to the flesh. The believer is a new creation (2 Cor. 5:17), and his new, incorruptible nature is patterned after the very nature of God Himself (2 Pet. 1:3-4). So believers will battle the flesh, which attempts to dominate, until the glorious redemption of their bodies.

2. Sin (v. 5*b*)

"The sinful impulses . . . did work in our members."

After discussing the flesh, Paul went on to say that man's unregenerate nature sends out sinful impulses to his body. The Greek word used for "work" (*energeō*) implies that the flesh energizes sin, which in turn generates more sin.

3. Law (v. 5c)

"Which were by the law."

How could God's perfect law create evil passion? It does so in two ways. First, because God's law is good, it exposes evil. If God's law hadn't been written upon the hearts of men, there would be no standard by which to judge evil. Second, nothing is more appealing to sinful man than to do something that is expressly forbidden. Simply tell people what they cannot do, and they will rush to disobey. The law of God both reveals and stimulates sin. Inherent within every man is a relentless effort to pursue evil.

4. Death (v. 5d)

"Bring forth fruit unto death."

The flesh produces sinful impulses, which are heightened and intensified by the law. The result is that which leads to death of both body and soul. It is an unfortunate and ungodly spiral downward.

IV. THE AFFIRMATION (v. 6)

A. The Deliverance (v. 6a)

"But now we are delivered from the law."

The phrase "but now" brings hope to this dismal scene of sin and death. Those who believe in Jesus Christ no longer serve the flesh because they have been released from the law. The law says man is guilty, and the penalty is death. However, Christ paid the penalty on our behalf so the law has no jurisdiction over those who place their faith in Him.

B. The Death (v. 6b)

"Being dead in which we were held."

Believers were once held captive to the flesh, which generated sin and led to death. But sin no longer reigns supreme

113

in the believer's life. Sin is no longer the master because its tyranny has been broken by Christ's death on the cross.

C. The Duty (v. 6c)

"That we should serve in newness of spirit and not in the oldness of the letter."

A question then arises: "Have believers therefore been set free to do whatever they want? Paul's answer is no. Believers have been delivered from the law to serve God. The Greek construction of this verse isn't saying that believers *should* serve but that they *will* serve. We have been saved not only to bear fruit (v. 4) but also to serve (v. 6). Kenneth Wuest translates this verse, "But now, we were discharged from the law, having died to that in which we were constantly held down, insomuch that we are rendering habitually a bondslave's obedience" (*Wuest's Word Studies from the Greek New Testament*, vol. 1 [Grand Rapids, Mich.: Eerdmans, 1973], p. 117).

1. The oldness of letter

Is grace going to make Christians sin? No. Grace transforms believers, producing security, holiness, liberty, fruitfulness, and service. Those are the marks of true saving faith. The service we render to God will not be "in the oldness of the letter" but "in newness of spirit." Our service is not submission to an external code or simply a mechanical obedience to religious ritual. It cannot be an external obedience to the law of God while the heart itself is unresponsive. That kind of response is pharisaical.

2. The newness of spirit

Believers serve God "in newness [Gk., *kainos*] of spirit." That refers to a new kind or quality of life, not new in terms of chronology. Our service to the Lord is internal and heartfelt.

When people question God's grace by saying it leads to sin, they simply do not understand what true salvation means. True salvation means that God plants an entirely new nature within the believer. And the bent of that new nature is to serve God from deep within the heart. Such service is energized by the Holy Spirit. That is why Paul said believers serve "in newness of *spirit*" (v. 6, emphasis added). Christians now serve the law better than ever because they have been redeemed. We are no longer slaves to a legal set of rules in an attempt to gain favor with God but now serve God out of love because He has granted us salvation by His grace.

Someone may ask, "Is the law binding on me now that I'm a Christian?" The answer is yes and no. It is not binding with regard to your right standing before God, but it is binding in that your new nature seeks to obey it. The law cannot save a man because he has no capacity to keep it, but now that God has saved you, you have the power to keep it for the first time in your life. Believers can declare along with the psalmist, "Oh, how I love thy law!" (Ps. 119:97).

Focusing on the Facts

1. True or false: According to Scripture, the law of God is a sinful thing, which is why believers should be free from it (see p. 97).
2. What is the whole duty of man? Support your answer with Scripture (see p. 98).
3. Where in the Old Testament do we read of the dignity and centrality of the law (see p. 99)?
4. What had the Jewish leaders done to the law of God (see p. 100)?
5. What was Paul's perception of the law of God before his conversion (see p. 101)?
6. How is God's law looked upon in the New Testament? Support your answer with Scripture (see p. 102).
7. True or false: Although God's law is sacred, holy, just, and good, it is utterly incapable of producing righteousness within sinful man (see p. 102).
8. How did Paul defend the grace of God (see p. 103)?
9. What is Paul's axiomatic principle in Romans 7:1 (see p. 103)?
10. What analogy did Paul use to describe his axiomatic principle (see p. 104)?
11. True or false: Paul's analogy in Romans 7:2-3 is a definitive statement on marriage, divorce, and remarriage (see p. 105).

12. _____ permanently ends the law that binds two people in marriage (see p. 106).

13. How did Jesus Christ satisfy the demands of God's law (see p. 107)?

14. Who is the believer ultimately married to? Support your answer with Scripture (see p. 108).

15. How secure is a believer in his relationship with Christ? Explain (see p. 108).

16. What is the underlying point in Romans (see p. 108)?

17. The purpose of any believer's life is to _____ God by bearing _____ (see p. 109).

18. What is the product of salvation? Explain (see p. 109).

19. What two kinds of fruit is Paul referring to in Romans 7:4? Explain using Scripture (see pp. 109-10).

20. What four key thoughts does the apostle Paul introduce in verse 5 (see pp. 110-13)?

21. What does Paul mean by his use of the word *flesh* in verse 5? In what ways is that term used in Scripture (see pp. 111-12)?

22. Are believers still living in the flesh? Explain why or why not (see p. 112).

23. What affirmation does Paul give in verse 6 regarding the believer and sin (see pp. 113-14)?

24. True believers do not serve the Lord in the_____ of _____ but in _____ of _____ (Rom. 7:6; see p. 114).

Pondering the Principles

1. Do you delight in the law of God? All the words in the Bible that refer to the law of God, which include "law," "testimony," "statutes," "commandments," and "ordinances," are synonymous with what is also referred to as the Word of God. Can you declare with the psalmist, "Oh, how I love thy law" (Ps. 119:97)? Over the next few months, read Psalm 19:7-10 and 119, asking God to give you love for His Word.

2. Jesus Christ satisfied the demands of the law by living a perfect life and then sacrificing His life on the cross (v. 4). Have you trusted in Christ as your Savior and Lord? That involves more than simply knowing the facts about Christ. It means beginning a personal relationship with Him. If you have not done so, repent from your sins, and receive Christ into your life. If you

have already done so, are you enjoying victory over sin? Are you bearing fruit for God? Pray that you might bear much fruit for Him, and seek ways to bring glory to His name.

7
Sin and the Law

Outline

Introduction
A. The Heart of the Gospel
   1. The destiny of man
   2. The desire of God
B. The Heart of the Epistle
   1. Established
   2. Explained
      a) The scriptural context
         (1) Romans 3
         (2) Romans 4
         (3) Romans 5
         (4) Romans 6
      b) The historical context
         (1) Objecting to lawlessness
         (2) Obeying the laws
            (*a*) The rabbinical corollaries
            (*b*) The scriptural consequences
            (*c*) The theological confrontation

Lesson
I. The Law Reveals Sin (v. 7)
   A. The Accusation Answered (v. 7*a*)
      1. Romans 3:20
      2. Romans 4:15
      3. Romans 5:13
   B. The Externals Examined (v. 7*b*)
      1. The experience of Paul's conviction
      2. The extent of Paul's tradition
         a) Galatians 1:13-14
         b) Philippians 3:5-6

Introduction

Romans 7:7-13 seems to be an intricate, complex, and difficult argument to understand at first reading. In that passage the apostle Paul says, "What shall we say then? Is the law sin? God forbid. Nay, I had not known sin but by the law; for I had not known coveting, except the law had said, Thou shalt not covet. But sin, taking occasion by the commandment, wrought in me all manner of coveting. For apart from the law sin is dead. For I was alive apart from the law once; but when the commandment came, sin revived, and I died. And the commandment, which was ordained to life, I found to be unto death. For sin, taking occasion by the commandment, deceived me, and by it slew me. Wherefore, the law is holy, and the commandment holy, and just, and good. Was then that which is good made death unto me? God forbid. But sin, that it might appear sin, working death in me by that which is good—that sin by the commandment might become exceedingly sinful."

A. The Heart of the Gospel

1. The destiny of man

Before we specifically examine the text, let me remind you of the greatest news ever known: Jesus Christ came into the world to save sinners. Because of sin, every member of the human race is bound for hell. That's because every person born into this world lives in rebellion against God and His divine law. And God, being a God of justice, must require punishment for such violation. Since man's crimes against God are so severe, there's no way he can ever pay for them.

2. The desire of God

Although hell is the destiny of man, it is not the desire of God's heart. Second Peter 3:9 says God is "not willing that any should perish, but that all should come to repentance." He sent Jesus Christ into the world to pay the debt that all men and women owe, to die the death that all should die, and to bear the sin that all should bear. He ordained that when men and women believe in Jesus Christ and accept His work on their behalf, their sin is forgiven forever, and they become partakers of His divine nature. So every believing sinner is equipped to spend eternity in heaven with God. That man can be made right with God and escape judgment is the best news that ever came into the world.

B. The Heart of the Epistle

The apostle Paul made justification by faith (that is, that men are made right with God through believing in the Lord Jesus Christ) the theme of his epistle to the Romans. It is also the central doctrine of the Christian faith.

1. Established

In Romans 1:16-17 Paul gives us the theme of the epistle: "I am not ashamed of the gospel of Christ; for it is

121

the power of God unto salvation to everyone that believeth; to the Jew first, and also to the [Gentile]. For in it is the righteousness of God revealed from faith to faith; as it is written, The just shall live by faith." The gospel tells us that salvation is available by grace through faith in Jesus Christ.

2. Explained

a) The scriptural context

Having established the theme, Paul unfolds the need for justification in the rest of chapters 1-2. He describes how it occurs in chapters 3-4. In chapters 5-8 he shows us the results of being justified by God's grace. One objection he anticipates in his discussion is that if you preach that works have no part in salvation or sanctification, then you're saying that people can do whatever they wish, and grace will cover everything. But Paul points out that justification by grace, rather than leading to license, leads to holiness, because inherent in justification is the impartation of divine life.

Grace and *faith* are key words that Paul uses in Romans 3-6.

(1) Romans 3—Verse 22 says, "The righteousness of God . . . is by *faith*." Verse 24 says we're "justified freely by his *grace*." Verse 25 says, "God hath set forth [Jesus Christ] to be a covering through *faith*." Verse 28 says, "Therefore, we conclude that a man is justified by *faith*." Verse 30 says, "Seeing it is one God, who shall justify the circumcision by *faith*, and the uncircumcision through *faith*."

(2) Romans 4—Verses 3-5 say, "What saith the scripture? Abraham believed God, and it was counted to him for righteousness. Now to him that worketh is the reward not reckoned of *grace*, but of debt, but to him that worketh not, but believeth on him that justifieth the ungodly, his *faith* is counted for righteousness." Verse 11 says Abra-

ham "received the sign of circumcision, a seal of the righteousness of the *faith* which he had." Verse 13 says, "The promise that he should be the heir of the world was not to Abraham, or to his seed, through the law, but through the righteousness of *faith*." Verse 16 says, "Therefore, it is of *faith*, that it might be *grace*." Verse 20 says Abraham "staggered not at the promise of God through unbelief, but was strong in *faith*."

(3) Romans 5—Verses 1-2 say we're "justified by *faith* [and] we have access by *faith* into this *grace*." Verses 20-21 say, "The law entered, that the offense might abound. But where sin abounded, *grace* did much more abound; that as sin hath reigned unto death, even so might *grace* reign through righteousness unto eternal life."

(4) Romans 6—Verse 23 says "the wages of sin is death, but the gift [grace] of God is eternal life through Jesus Christ, our Lord."

b) The historical context

(1) Objecting to lawlessness

Paul's message of grace and faith was unique in its historical context. The Jewish people had been told that you please God by obeying His rules and conforming to His standards. Although that is true, they had gradually come to believe that you must work your way into God's good favor. So when Paul preached that salvation is a free gift that can't be earned because it is received by faith (which itself is a gift of God, Eph. 2:8-9), his message was difficult for many of the Jewish people to accept. They were committed to the law of God and to a works-righteousness system. They accused Paul of advocating lawlessness. Since they believed the law procured and maintained a person's holiness, they assumed that if it was taken away, then the safeguard to holiness would be eliminated. All they could see was society running amok under Paul's teaching of grace.

123

(2) Obeying the laws

    (*a*) The rabbinical corollaries

The law of God is commonly divided into three parts: the ceremonial law, the social law, and the moral law. The Jews believed you had to keep all of those laws to become holy. By the time of Paul's ministry, the rabbis had summed up all of the Old Testament law in 613 commandments. But it was almost impossible to keep them all, especially since they had been embellished beyond the intention of God.

The rabbis divided the 613 laws into mandatory things that had to be done and prohibitory things that could not be done. They taught there were 248 things you had to do that related to God, the Temple, sacrifices, vows, rituals, donations, the Sabbath, diet, festivals, community, idolatry, war, social issues, family, judicial matters, legal rights, and slaves.

The 365 prohibitory laws related to idolatry, historical lessons, blasphemy, Temple worship, sacrifices, priests, diet, vows, agriculture, loans, business, slaves, justice, and relationships. Those laws had all kinds of corollaries and adjunct laws to the point that keeping the law was a burdensome way of life. That's why Peter mentioned that the law was "a yoke . . . which neither our fathers nor we were able to bear" (Acts 15:10).

    (*b*) The scriptural consequences

Scripture itself instilled in the Jewish people the need to obey the law. Deuteronomy 27:26 says, "Cursed be he who confirmeth not all the words of this law to do them." The next chapter warns of severe consequences for not obeying: "But it shall come to pass, if thou wilt not hearken unto the voice of the Lord thy God, to observe to do all his commandments and his statutes which I command thee this day, that all these curses shall come upon thee, and overtake thee. Cursed shalt thou be in the city, and cursed shalt thou be in the field. Cursed shall be thy basket and thy kneading-trough. Cursed shall be the fruit of thy body, and the fruit of thy land, the increase of thy cows, and the flocks of thy sheep. Cursed shalt thou be when thou comest in, and cursed shalt thou be when thou goest out. The Lord shall send upon thee cursing, vexation, and rebuke, in all that thou settest thine hand to do, until thou be destroyed, and until thou perish quickly, because of the wickedness of thy doings, whereby thou hast forsaken me. The Lord shall make the pestilence cling unto thee, until he have consumed thee from off the land, to which thou goest to possess it. The Lord shall smite thee with a consumption, and with a fever, and with an inflammation, and with an extreme burning, and with the sword, and with blight, and with mildew; and they shall pursue thee until thou perish" (28:15-22).

That's a fairly comprehensive curse—and that's not even the end of it! It continues through the rest of the chapter, extending its way through every conceivable dimension of life. Is it any wonder the Jewish people felt so bound to the law? It was, after all, the law of God, and neither the law nor its Author were open to debate.

The apostle Paul alludes to the burden of the law in his epistles. He, too, must have borne that burden, having once been a zealous Pharisee (Phil. 3:5-6). In Galatians 3:10 he says, "As many as are of the works of the law are under the curse." Those who are trying to please God by keeping the law are under a curse. Why? Because no one can keep the law perfectly. In the same verse he quotes Deuteronomy 27:26: "Cursed is everyone that continueth not in all things which are written in the book of the law, to do them." That tells us Paul understood what Deuteronomy was saying.

(c) The theological confrontation

When Paul said that no one shall be justified by the deeds of the law (Gal. 3:11), he was stamping on the theological toes of those who found that conclusion difficult to accept. He confronted them with the utter futility of trying to keep the law, stating in the same verse that "no man is justified by the law in the sight of God, it is evident; for the just shall live by faith" (quoted from Hab. 2:4). So the Old Testament said that man was cursed if he failed to keep the law. James knew that. He said, "Whosoever shall keep the whole law, and yet offend in one point, he is guilty of all" (James 2:10).

Why Did God Give Israel a Law They Couldn't Keep?

God gave Israel a law they couldn't keep to show them how sinful they were and to drive them to Himself by faith. But the Israelites didn't want to come to God by faith. Content with their self-righteousness, they believed they could merit God's favor on their own. So they were all under a curse.

To break one law of God is not like breaking one spoke in a bicycle wheel and continuing to ride. It's more like breaking a pane of glass —you break the pane in one spot, and it shatters. Because Israel couldn't keep the law and refused to come to God by faith, they were under the curse of the law.

Romans 6:14 says, "Sin shall not have dominion over you; for ye are not under the law but under grace." Believers are no longer under

126

the curse of the law. Christ was made a curse for us that we might be set free from the curse of the law (Gal. 3:13).

At this point a question arises: If the law can't save us (Rom. 3-4) or sanctify us (Rom. 5-6) and is nothing but a curse, then what good is it? If we're saved and made holy by our union with Christ, what place does the law have? Why did God go to such extremes to give such a complex law? Paul answers those questions in Romans 7.

The Role of the Law

Paul has been building up to an explanation of the law's place since chapter 3, when he first mentioned that the law couldn't save us. Chapters 3-8 give us a comprehensive view of the law and its role. In this section we learn some important things about the law:

- It can't save us (Rom. 3-5).
- It can't make us holy (Rom. 6).
- It can't condemn us if we're in Christ (Rom. 7:1-6).
- It can convict us of sin (Rom. 7:7-13).
- It can't deliver us from sin (Rom. 7:14-25).
- It can be fulfilled in the power of the indwelling Spirit (Rom. 8:1-4).

Lesson

Romans 7:7-13 answers the question, If the law can't save us or sanctify us, what good is it? This passage teaches us that it is good because it can convict us in four ways.

I. THE LAW REVEALS SIN (v. 7)

A. The Accusation Answered (v. 7*a*)

"What shall we say then? Is the law sin? God forbid. Nay."

Paul anticipated the Jewish antagonist who would say, "You've just said we're dead to the law, which has been set

127

aside. If we're out from under the authority of that which was trying to condemn us, are you saying that the law God gave to His people was evil?"

Paul's answer was the strongest negative in the Greek language: "God forbid" (*mē genoito*). He was saying, "No, no, no! The law cannot be considered evil under any circumstance. That would be an utter absurdity!" In verse 7 he goes on to say he would not have recognized his sin unless the law had revealed it. We are not to be saved by the law, but we are to be convicted by it.

If there weren't any law, there wouldn't be any sin. For example, without a sign saying, "Keep Off the Grass," there would be nothing wrong with standing on the grass. Similarly, if there's no law about driving a certain speed, you can legally drive as fast as your car will carry you. However, once the standard is established, you are responsible for not violating it. Breaking God's law reveals sin.

1. Romans 3:20—"Therefore, by the deeds of the law there shall be no flesh be justified in his sight; for by the law is the knowledge of sin." That's an important truth. The law simply shows us what sin is by God's definition.

2. Romans 4:15—"Where no law is, there is no transgression."

3. Romans 5:13—"Sin is not imputed when there is no law."

Chapters 3, 4, and 5 say the same thing: without a law you don't have sin. So when God reveals the law, we immediately are measured by the standard and are found to be sinners.

B. The Externals Examined (v. 7*b*)

"I had not known sin but by the law."

1. The experience of Paul's conviction

Paul is saying, "I never knew the full extent of my sin until I understood the full extent of the law. When I understood the law, I felt convicted of sin." Paul's use of the first-person singular means he is giving a personal testimony of what was going on in his own heart. I believe the recognition of his personal sinfulness was part of the convicting work of the Spirit of God on the Damascus road and the days of blindness that followed. That experience forced him to come to grips with his own life and see his need for a Savior.

I believe it's important that Scripture records that part of Paul's spiritual journey, because if we knew only the confrontation on the Damascus road, we might think he was saved apart from his own will. If he was persecuting Christians at one point and then was suddenly ordained to the ministry, you wouldn't know whether there was any personal conviction involved in his salvation. But Romans 7:7-13 reveals that God was progressively convicting Paul's heart of sin as he began to see the law of God for what it was.

2. The extent of Paul's tradition

For a long time Paul thought he knew all about the law of God. He was a Pharisee and had spent his life trying to keep the law. He had previously been in the category of people he later describes in Romans 10:2-3 as having "a zeal for God, but not according to knowledge. . . . being ignorant of God's righteousness, and going about to establish their own righteousness." He was like the Pharisee in Luke 18 who said, "God, I thank thee that I am not as other men are. . . . I fast twice in the week; I give tithes of all that I possess" (vv. 11-12).

a) Galatians 1:13-14—In writing to the Galatians, Paul said, "Ye have heard of my manner of life in time past in the Jews' religion how that beyond measure I profited in the Jews' religion, above many my equals in mine own nation, being more exceedingly zealous of the traditions of my fathers." Paul's reputation as a zealous Jewish leader had spread far and wide. He once boasted of his religious zeal in keeping the law.

b) Philippians 3:5-6—Paul gives a similar testimony with more detail, stating he was "circumcised on the eighth day, of the stock of Israel, of the tribe of Benjamin, an Hebrew of the Hebrews; as touching the law, a Pharisee; concerning zeal, persecuting the church; as touching the righteousness which is in the law, blameless." Do you want to know how he could say that? The same way the rich young man could admit to the Lord that he had kept all the law since his youth (Matt. 19:20). Such people have a limited understanding of the law of God and its internal implications. They reinterpret it to accommodate their sinfulness so they can maintain the appearance of external righteousness and assume they are acceptable to God.

However, when Paul recognized his spiritual depravity, he admitted that mere external righteousness is of no more value than manure (v. 8). Once he got a view of where the real problem was—on the inside, where the law really needed to be applied, he saw what he was.

C. The Internalization Implied (v. 7c)

"For I had not known coveting [Gk., *epithumia*, "lusting" or "evil desire"], except the law had said, Thou shalt not covet."

Romans 7:7-13 records the conviction Paul experienced before he was saved. Note what illustration he chose out of all the Ten Commandments. Paul selected a commandment that relates solely to a person's motivation. Coveting isn't an external act; it's something that happens internally. Paul was saying, "When I realized that the law of God had to do not just with my acts but with my attitudes, like lusting for what isn't mine, I realized that all my self-righteous actions were worthless because I was filled with vile desires." That's true conviction of sin.

1. Concentrating on externals

  a) Superficial conviction

    When some people recognize their need to get their life right, they limit the changes to externals like lying, getting drunk, or getting angry. It's good to

130

avoid those things, but they don't understand that the real issue of sin is internal. They might be able to control their actions through means other than grace. By going to Alcoholics Anonymous they might stop their drinking problem. By going to a psychologist they might stop their lying. There are many ways to reform one's actions. However, the only way the evil desire of a person's heart will be cleared is by divine transformation.

b) Sincere conviction

The law was intended to stimulate that transformation by bringing about conviction. That's why there aren't just external commands but internal ones as well. They hit with the greatest impact. Not only was that Paul's experience, but it is for all who come to true conviction. I believe that when you come to Jesus Christ, you realize that not only do you have trouble controlling the outside, but you even have worse trouble controlling the inside.

Theologian Charles Hodge said, "The law, although it cannot secure either the justification or sanctification of men, performs an essential part in the economy of salvation. It enlightens conscience and secures its verdict against a multitude of evils, which we should not otherwise have recognized as sins. It arouses sin, increasing its power, and making it, both in itself and in our consciousness, exceedingly sinful. It therefore produces that state of mind which is a necessary preparation for the reception of the gospel. . . . Conviction of sin, that is, an adequate knowledge of its nature, and a sense of its power over us, is an indispensable part of evangelical religion. Before the gospel can be embraced as a means of deliverance from sin, we must feel we are involved in corruption and misery" (*Commentary on the Epistle to the Romans* [Grand Rapids, Mich.: Eerdmans, n.d.], p. 226).

2. Condemning externals

Apart from the law, people don't recognize their sinfulness. It's not unusual to hear someone say, "I'm not such a bad guy. God certainly wouldn't send a good person like me to hell; I do my very best. I try to do what's right and obey the laws." Many people live under that illusion. But that must be changed if you're to be saved. Even though on the outside you may have control of your life and look like the citizen of the century, in the words of Jesus you "are like whited sepulchers, which indeed appear beautiful outward, but are within full of dead men's bones" (Matt. 23:27).

Let's examine Matthew 5 to see how our Lord proclaimed the convicting message of salvation to His Jewish audience. In verses 21-22 He says, "Ye have heard it that it was said by them of old, Thou shalt not kill and whosoever shall kill shall be in danger of judgment. But I say unto you that whosoever is angry with his brother without a cause shall be in danger of judgment." The rabbinic tradition had lowered God's standards to fulfilling a bunch of external requirements, but Jesus reinstated God's intention by saying that the attitude of hatred is as much a sin as the act of murder. Similarly He said, "Ye have heard that it was said by them of old, Thou shalt not commit adultery; but I say unto you that whosoever looketh on a woman to lust after her hath committed adultery with her already in his heart" (vv. 27-28). In verses 33-34 Jesus says, "Ye have heard that it hath been said by them of old, Thou shalt not perjure thyself . . . but I say unto you, Swear not at all." Jewish tradition had degenerated to the point that if a person swore by certain things, he didn't have to mean it. It was another indication of the externalized religion they had created. Therefore, the Lord identified the root problem as going beyond acts like murder and adultery, for He focused on the internal sins like hatred and lust.

In bringing men to conviction, Jesus had to show them that the law of God touches the inside of man, not just the outside. That's why when asked by a lawyer how to inherit eternal life, Jesus taught that he must love the Lord God with all his heart, soul, strength, and mind and his neighbor as himself (Luke 10:25-28). Does it sound easy to love God with your whole being by seeking His glory in everything you do and to seek the good will and benefit of others? Those two simple concepts summarize the whole law and place the responsibility inside.

In Romans 7 we learn that Paul internalized God's law around the time of his conversion. When he saw the wretchedness of his covetous heart, he knew what a sinner he was. He saw that the law condemned the sinful desires of his heart. Likewise, people who think they are moral must look deeper and discover the wretchedness of their hearts before they can come to Christ. So the intention of the law is to show sin for what it really is—deep corruption of the inner nature of man.

II. THE LAW AROUSES SIN (v. 8)

"But sin, taking occasion by the commandment, wrought in me all manner of coveting. For apart from the law sin is dead."

A. The Dormancy of Sin (v. 8b)

"Apart from the law sin is dead."

That verse is not saying that sin doesn't exist; we know it does. The idea is that until you see the law of God in its fullness, sin is dead to you in the sense that it doesn't overwhelm you. You are not fully aware of it. Only when the law of God floods your heart and shows you what sin really is can you come to Christ.

Some people justify their sin by admitting that it's wrong to commit atrocities like murder. Perhaps they point to the sin they find in other people's lives. They may even want to improve their own lives. But they don't understand the profound depth of sin as something that will condemn them to eternal hell. They don't see the wretchedness of sin until someone comes before them with the law of God.

B. The Development of Sin (v. 8*a*)

"But sin, taking occasion by the commandment, wrought in me all manner of coveting."

The Greek term translated "occasion" (*aphormē*) was used in a military sense to refer to a base of operations from which an attack is launched. Sin is launched by the law. As soon as a commandment of God enters in, sin takes over.

Be a Bad-News Bearer

The Puritans preached the law before they preached the gospel to bring people to a point of desperation so they could recognize their need for a Savior. You can't waltz people into the kingdom through positive thinking. You can't merely ask, "Wouldn't you like to be happy and experience peace and joy?" Who wouldn't? Any thinking person would eagerly reply, "Where do I sign?" Unfortunately, they wouldn't even know what they're signing for. In contrast, the Bible always presents the bad news about man's vile nature before it offers the good news of salvation. If people try to keep the law and earn their way to heaven without admitting their sin, they'll fall deeper into the curse. In getting out from under the law, they must believe in the Lord Jesus Christ and recognize their utter moral bankruptcy before a holy God and their inability to save themselves.

1. The problem identified

The law is not the culprit for man being cursed—sin is. The law does us good by exposing sin. Only then can we see our need for a Savior. We can't preach half the message.

Commentator F. F. Bruce writes, "The villain of the piece is Sin; Sin seized the opportunity afforded it when the law showed me what was right and what was wrong" (*The Epistle of Paul to the Romans* [Grand Rapids, Mich.: Eerdmans, 1963], p. 150). Our real problem is sin, not the law. That is what explains the weakness of the law to save us. The law cannot save us because we cannot keep it, and we cannot keep it because of in-dwelling sin.

Galatians 3:21 says, "Is the law, then, against the promises of God? God forbid; for if there had been a law given which could have given life, verily righteousness should have been by the law." If keeping the law was designed to result in salvation, then it would have been able to impart righteousness. But it couldn't, not because there was something wrong with the law, but because there was something wrong with the people.

2. The problem intensified

Not only does the law of God reveal sin for what it is so that you become more aware of its existence, but also it stimulates and increases your desire to do what is wrong. If you emphatically tell a person not to do something, he is much more tempted to do it than if you had said nothing.

Bible scholar John Murray says in his book *Principles of Conduct* that the more the light of the law shines in our depraved hearts, the more the enmity of our minds is aroused to opposition, proving that the mind of the flesh is not subject to the law of God ([Grand Rapids, Mich.: Eerdmans, 1957], p. 185). When confronted with the holy law of God, man doesn't find himself eager to obey it; he finds himself aggravated to an even greater extent to disobey it. That shows how depraved we are. In Romans 7:14-25 the apostle Paul speaks from the perspective of a believer. He is naturally drawn to do right—he realizes that something in him longs to obey the law of God, yet he is aggravated by that same law to do wrong. So the law reveals and arouses sin.

III. THE LAW DEVASTATES THE SINNER (vv. 9-11)

A. The Process of Devastation (v. 9)

"For I was alive apart from the law once; but when the commandment came, sin revived, and I died."

1. Explained

Paul doesn't mean he was spiritually alive before the law became clear to him; he means he was doing fine. He was content with his self-righteous life. But when he was exposed to the convicting power of the law, he died in the sense that everything he hoped in was shattered. He lost his sense of security and self-satisfaction. He was devastated when he saw the extent of God's law and recognized that his own sinfulness made it impossible for him to save himself. In terms of the Beatitudes, Paul was poor in spirit and mournful over his sin (Matt. 5:3-5). He recognized he was "without strength" (Rom. 5:6) and in need of a divine physician (Matt. 9:12). He was searching for a way out of the horrendous guilt that came as a result of being exposed to the law.

How to Evaluate the Genuineness of Your Salvation

You evaluate your salvation not by your reaction to God's love but by your reaction to God's law. It's not a matter of feeling good about yourself but of feeling bad about yourself. We demonstrate that we truly love others when we care enough to confront their sin. That's why we have to reaffirm the law of God. God wants the law to devastate the sinner by knocking him flat on his back.

2. Exemplified

I read of an experiment in which scientists discovered that when they filled a balloon with warm water and brought it near a coiled rattlesnake, the snake would feel the heat of the balloon and strike it, releasing its poisonous venom. In the same way as the balloon provided occasion for release of the poison, the law of God provides release for the venom of man's sin.

In *The Pilgrim's Progress*, John Bunyan pictures the law's function of aggravating the sinner. The pilgrim, Christian, is taken into a large room, which represents the heart. The room is full of dust, symbolizing sin. When a man with a broom, representing the law, begins to sweep, he stirs up so much dust that Christian almost suffocates. The law does just that: it enters your life and stirs up sin, enabling you to see it and seek a remedy in Jesus Christ.

B. The Purpose of the Commandments (v. 10)

"And the commandment, which was ordained to life, I found to be unto death."

The law was given to provide blessedness in life by leading those who observed it to a full, meaningful, and joyous life (Prov. 3:1-2). God abundantly blesses obedience by enriching the quality of a person's life. The law of God was ordained to produce a blessed life of godliness with contentment (1 Tim. 6:6). It was designed to regulate men in the path of righteousness and thus promote life.

However, it cannot accomplish that purpose in an unsaved person because he doesn't have the ability to obey the law and therefore receive its benefits of blessing. So Paul was saying that the law, instead of giving him a rich and meaningful life, devastated him.

In what sense can the law give life? If you're a Christian—if you love the Lord Jesus Christ and the Holy Spirit dwells within you—the Spirit will help you fulfill the law. Romans 8:4 says God designed "that the righteousness of the law might be fulfilled in us, who walk not after the flesh, but after the Spirit." If you obey God in the power of the Spirit (which you can do only if you're a Christian), God will bless and prosper your life as He pours out His grace upon it. He will enable you to live life to its fullest, a life characterized by happiness and holiness. But when God's law confronts an unregenerate person, all it does is show him how evil he is and make him miserable. The unsaved cannot expect to receive salvation or sanctification from the law. That was the devastating frustration Paul once experienced. The law of God revealed that what he once believed was valuable in life was only dung, or refuse (Phil. 3:8).

C. The Deception of Sin (v. 11)

"For sin, taking occasion by the commandment, deceived me, and by it slew me."

1. The experience of Paul in particular

Paul reiterated that sin killed him when the law convicted him. He had been deceived into thinking he was blameless as he went about persecuting Christians in his zeal for God. He was a member of the religious leadership of Israel and probably assumed God was pleased with him. In today's terminology, he thought he had his act together. But then he was confronted with the reality of God's holy law. He looked inside and saw the evil in his heart. He realized that all the religious things he had been doing couldn't help him, so he threw himself on the mercy of Jesus Christ.

Sin deceived him in that it led him to expect one thing while he was experiencing another. He thought that if he was righteous in himself, he'd find true blessing and purpose in life. But all he got was the misery, unhappiness, disillusionment, and disappointment of sin.

2. The expectations of people in general

The world is filled with people like Paul. They are madly pursuing a religion that promotes self-righteousness through various rules and rituals. They may prayerfully repeat certain formulas, light candles, visit shrines, or attend seminars. Many people belong to religions that teach if they do certain things, live a good life, and don't do prohibited things, then they will experience blessing in this life and earn the right to enter heaven, attain godhood, or some other reward after death. Such people are deceived. If they examined their hearts they might realize that they're not alive at all and that the promises their religious system has made to them will remain unfulfilled. Sin deceives them into thinking they can find happiness apart from God's truth, but all they find is misery, unhappiness, and death.

Paul once thought all desirable spiritual goals were available through the law, but when he learned the truth, he knew he had been deceived. Millions are similarly deceived. The deceitfulness of sin makes people believe they can please God and gain His blessing by their good works alone. But that is a lie.

Scripture warns us of the deceitfulness of sin. Ephesians 4:22 says, "Put off concerning the former manner of life the old man, which is corrupt according to the deceitful lusts." Hebrews 3:13 says, "Exhort one another daily, while it is called Today, lest any of you be hardened through the deceitfulness of sin."

IV. THE LAW REFLECTS THE SINFULNESS OF SIN (vv. 12-13)

A. The Character of the Law (v. 12)

"Wherefore, the law is holy, and the commandment holy, and just, and good."

How can the law be holy, just, and good since Paul just said it arouses sin and devastates the sinner? Paul's answer is the key to this chapter. He tells us the law is spiritual (v. 14) and good (v. 16), and that he "delights in the law" (v. 22). There is nothing wrong with the law. If the law reveals sin, it isn't the law that is at fault. If a person is convicted for murder and given the death penalty, do you blame the law for convicting him? No. It isn't even the lawyers, the judge, or the jury that ultimately sentences him; it's the law. The purpose of a court is to uphold the law. Anyone who defies the law is at fault.

1. It is holy

   The law is as pure as God is pure. Since God is perfect, it follows logically that the standard He reveals will also be perfect.

2. It is just

   The law is just, meaning it is equitable, fair, or right. There's nothing wrong or unjust about the law.

3. It is good

   The law promotes blessing. But how could the law, which has caused sin to flourish, promote the good of man? Because where sin flourishes or abounds, grace abounds that much more (Rom. 5:20). The law reveals we are sinners in need of a Savior. When we run to the Savior, we find grace.

Psalm 19 says, "The law of the Lord is perfect, converting the soul; the testimony of the Lord is sure, making wise the simple. The statutes of the Lord are right, rejoicing the heart; the commandment of the Lord is pure, enlightening the eyes. The fear of the Lord is clean, enduring forever; the ordinances of the Lord are true and righteous altogether. More to be desired are they than gold, yea, than much fine gold; sweeter also than honey and the honeycomb. Moreover, by them is thy servant warned: and in keeping of them there is great reward" (vv. 7-11). The law of God has a wonderful purpose: it converts the soul, gives wisdom, and reveals the truth. It's not the law that's at fault; it's the man.

B. The Cause of Death (v. 13)

"Was then that which is good made death unto me? God forbid. But sin, that it might appear sin, working death in me by that which is good—that sin by the commandment might become exceedingly sinful."

So does the law deserve the blame for our sin? We've established that when a criminal is convicted, the law is not to blame. The law simply exposes sin. The law isn't what is deadly; sin is. The law was given to produce abundant life. Just because man can't live up to it doesn't mean that it is bad. Paul emphasizes that the law reveals sin. The phrase "but sin that it might appear sin" tells us sin's true character is exposed when you understand the law of God. That is why we must preach against sin.

When the law unmasks our sin, it brings about death by showing us how far short we fall of God's perfect standards. That leads the thinking man to echo the words of Paul: "Oh, wretched man that I am!" (Rom. 7:24). Or, in the words of the tax collector in Luke 18, "God be merciful to me a sinner" (v. 13).

Paul's argument is powerful. The law is holy, just, and good even though it reveals sin, aggravates it, and uses sin to devastate the sinner. It demonstrates the exceeding sinfulness of sin. If sin can use the law of God—which is holy, just, and good—to produce such terrible effects, twisting and perverting something that is pure, it must be treacherous. But the law is not at fault; sin is. Men are so evil that instead of realizing the holy purpose of God's law they oppose it. They are deceived into believing that they can indulge in sin without consequence. In stark contrast are the good works of the law in driving us to despair—leading to salvation—and the utter sinfulness of sin in using something as holy as the law of God to work death in us.

Conclusion

In Galatians 3 Paul says, "Wherefore, then, serveth the law? It was added because of transgressions, till the seed [Messiah] should come" (v. 19). The law was given that men might face their sin and recognize their need for a Savior.

Paul continues, "Is the law, then, against the promises of God? God forbid. . . . The scripture [i.e., the law], hath concluded all under sin, that the promise by faith of Jesus Christ might be given to them that believe. But before faith came, we were kept under the law, shut up unto the faith which should afterwards be revealed. Wherefore, the law was our schoolmaster [tutor] to bring us unto Christ, that we might be justified by faith" (vv. 21-24). The main purpose of the law was to bring us to Christ that we might be justified by faith.

Robert Murray McCheyne died in 1843 at the age of thirty, but he left a lasting mark on Christendom. He wrote "Jehovah Tsidkenu," which means "the Lord our righteousness":

> I once was a stranger to grace and to God,
> I know not my danger, and felt not my load;
> Though friends spoke in rapture of Christ on the tree,
> Jehovah Tsidkenu was nothing to me.

I oft read with pleasure, to soothe or engage,
Isaiah's wild measure and John's simple page;
But even when they pictured the blood-sprinkled tree,
Jehovah Tsidkenu seemed nothing to me.

Like tears from the daughters of Zion that roll,
I wept when the waters went over His soul,
Yet thought not that my sins had nailed to the tree
Jehovah Tsidkenu—'twas nothing to me.

When free grace awoke me by light from on high,
Then legal fears shook me, I trembled to die;
No refuge, no safety in self could I see—
Jehovah Tsidkenu my Savior must be.

My terrors all vanished before the sweet name;
My guilty fear banished, with boldness I came
To drink at the fountain, life-giving and free—
Jehovah Tsidkenu is all things to me.

Jehovah Tsidkenu! my treasure and boast,
Jehovah Tsidkenu! I ne'er can be lost;
In Thee shall I conquer by flood and by field—
My cable, my anchor, my breastplate and shield!
Even treading the valley, the shadow of death,
This "watchword" shall rally my faltering breath;
For while from life's fever my God sets me free,
Jehovah Tsidkenu my death-song shall be.

Robert Murray McCheyne experienced the same conviction that the apostle Paul did. When exposed to the light of God's law, he died a ruinous death. But out of the ashes came a redemptive faith in the Lord Jesus Christ. The law cannot save us or sanctify us, but the law can convict us of sin and lead us to Christ.

There's instruction here for the Christian also. When you came to Christ, you came because you saw your sin for what it was and cried out to Him. The law still has that function in your life. We need constant exposure to the holy standards of God so we can identify the sin in our lives and deal with it—not to maintain our salvation but our fellowship with God. Only then will we experience the full blessing that belongs to God's children. As you study the Word of God, let it remind you of the standard so that you may regularly cry out in humble repentance before God.

When the psalmist said, "Thy word have I hidden in mine heart, that I might not sin against thee" (Ps. 119:11), he may have been indicating that he regularly exposed himself to God's law so he would recognize the sin in his life and turn from it. May we follow his example.

Focusing on the Facts

1. What is the greatest news ever known (see p. 121)?
2. Although hell is man's destiny, what is God's desire? Support your answer with Scripture (see p. 121).
3. What allows a sinner to spend eternity with God (see p. 121)?
4. What doctrine is the main theme of Romans (see p. 121)?
5. What does justification by grace lead people to? Why (see p. 122)?
6. Identify two keys words Paul uses consistently in Romans 3-6 (see p. 122).
7. Why was Paul's message of grace and faith unique in its immediate historical context (see p. 123)?
8. Of what did Jewish people accuse Paul (see p. 123)?
9. What are three parts of God's law? How did the rabbis divide the law? Why did the Jewish people feel compelled to keep that tradition (see p. 124)?
10. According to Scripture, what were the consequences for failing to observe God's law (see pp. 124-25)?
11. Why are those who try to please God and gain salvation by keeping the law under a curse (see pp. 125-26)?
12. Explain why God gave Israel a law that they couldn't keep (see p. 126).
13. Why are believers no longer under the curse of the law (Gal. 3:13; see pp. 126-27)?
14. Match the particular role of the law with the appropriate passage (see p. 127):

It can't condemn us if we're in Christ.	Romans 7:14-25
It can be fulfilled through the Spirit.	Romans 7:1-6
It can't save us.	Romans 6
It can't make us holy.	Romans 3-5
It can't deliver us from sin.	Romans 7:7-13
It can convict us of sin.	Romans 8:1-4

15. For what hypothetical question does Romans 7:7-13 provide the answer (Rom. 7:7; see p. 127)?
16. Can a violation exist without a law's prohibiting it? Give an example, and support your conclusion with Scripture (see p. 128).
17. We are not to be _____ by the law, but we are to be _____ by it (see p. 128).
18. Describe Paul's zeal before his conversion (see pp. 129-30).
19. How was it possible for Paul and the rich young ruler of Matthew 19:20 to believe they had blamelessly kept the law (see p. 130)?
20. What kind of changes do most people make when they want to get their lives right? What is the only way the evil desires of a person's heart will be cleaned up (see pp. 130-31)?
21. What's the difference between superficial and sincere conviction (see pp. 130-31)?
22. What had rabbinical tradition done with God's standards? What did Jesus show the people about God's law (see pp. 132-33)?
23. How do some people justify their sin (see p. 133)?
24. Why did the Puritans preach about the law before they preached the gospel (see p. 134)?
25. The _____ is not the culprit; _____ is (Rom. 7:8; see p. 134).
26. How does the law intensify sin? What does that show about the nature of man (see p. 135)?
27. What did Paul mean when he said he "was alive apart from the law once" (Rom. 7:9; p. 136)?
28. In *The Pilgrim's Progress*, what do the room, the dust, and the man with the broom represent (see pp. 136-37)?
29. In what sense were God's commandments ordained to bring life? Could they accomplish that purpose in an unsaved person? Explain (see p. 137).
30. How did sin deceive Paul (see p. 138)?
31. What does the deceitfulness of sin make people believe they can do (see p. 138)?
32. How does Paul describe the law in Romans 7:12? Explain why the law doesn't deserve the blame for our sin (see pp. 139-40)?
34. Explain how the law promotes man's blessedness (see p. 139).
35. According to Galatians 3:19-24, why was the law given (see p. 141)?

Pondering the Principles

1. If you were asked why you should be allowed to enter heaven, what would you say? Have you let Jesus Christ pay the debt for your sin, or are you trying to pay that debt yourself through good works? If you have already believed the good news that Jesus did for you what you yourself could never do, are you sharing that good news with others?

2. The world is eager to believe that God is loving, but it is not so willing to believe that His holy standards are far higher than man can reach. Prideful man is not naturally willing to humble himself before a holy God, yet conviction of sin is an essential part of the salvation process. Are you including the holiness of God and the sinfulness of man in your presentation of the gospel to others? Pray that those you tell the gospel to would see the depth of their sin—which extends beyond the actions to the heart—and turn to Christ.

3. God blesses obedience to Him by enriching the quality of a person's life. Do you see evidence of God's blessing in your life? If so, meditate on Psalm 103, and give the thanks for all He has given you. If, however, you find an absence of blessing, consider whether any disobedience to God's Word has contributed to that result. If you feel you are stuck in a spiritual rut—spinning your wheels but going nowhere—meditate on John 15:1-11, and evaluate whether you are abiding in Christ.

4. Christians need to constantly expose themselves to God's holy standards so that they can recognize sin in their lives. Are you reading God's Word on a regular basis? Are you going to church to hear the Word taught? Are you evaluating your life by God's standards, or are you comparing yourself with others? Make sure you confess your sins as soon as you become aware of them so that you may continue to experience the blessings that belongs to God's children. Read Psalm 32, and determine whether you can identify with David's insights.

8

The Believer and Indwelling Sin—Part 1

Outline

Introduction
A. The Controversy over the Passage
    1. The non-Christian view
        a) Supporting its position
            (1) The power of the Spirit
            (2) The peace of God
            (3) The freedom of believers
        b) Stating its problems
    2. The Christian view
        a) The accurate description of a Christian
            (1) Pursuing God
            (2) Hating sin
        b) The acute debate over carnality
            (1) The Christian of Romans 7 is spiritual immature
            (2) The Christian of Romans 7 is spiritually mature
                (a) Paul's confessions throughout Scripture
                    i)   1 Corinthians 15:9-10
                    ii)   Ephesians 3:8
                    iii) 1 Timothy 1:12-16
                (b) Paul's emphasis through Romans 7
                    i)   The terms he uses
                    ii)   The transitions he makes
B. The Context of the Passage

Lesson
I. The Struggle Recorded (vv. 14-23)
    A. The First Lament (vv. 14-17)
        1. The condition of carnality (v. 14)
            a) The affirmation of spirituality
            b) The admission of sinfulness

Introduction

Romans 7:14-25 says, "We know that the law is spiritual; but I am carnal, sold under sin. For that which I do I understand not; for what I would, that do I not; but what I hate, that do I. If, then, I do that which I would not, I consent unto the law that it is good. Now, then, it is no more I that do it, but sin that dwelleth in me. For I know that in me (that is, in my flesh) dwelleth no good thing; for to will is present with me, but how to perform that which is good I find not. For the good that I would, I do not; but the evil which I would not, that I do. Now if I do that I would not, it is no more I that do it, but sin that dwelleth in me. I find then a law, that, when I would do good, evil is present with me. For I delight in the law of God after the inward man; but I see another law in my members, warring against the law of my mind, and bringing me into captivity to the law of sin which is in my members. Oh, wretched man that I am! Who shall deliver me from the body of this death? I thank God through Jesus Christ, our Lord. So, then, with the mind I myself serve the law of God; but with the flesh, the law of sin."

That passage is a poignant description of someone in conflict with himself—someone who loves God's moral law and wants to obey it but is pulled away from doing so by the sin that is in him. It is the personal experience of a soul in conflict. This intense warfare within the heart is summed up in the desperate cry of verse 24, "Oh, wretched man that I am! Who shall deliver me?"

A. The Controversy over the Passage

There has always been debate whether Paul was describing a Christian or a non-Christian in this passage. Some people

148

say there is too much bondage to sin in view for this passage to refer to a Christian. Others say there is too much desire to do good for a non-Christian. You can't be a Christian and be bound to sin, and you can't be a non-Christian and desire to keep the law of God. Therein is the conflict of interpreting the passage.

1. The non-Christian view

    a) Supporting its position

        (1) The power of the Spirit

        Those who believe Romans 7:14-25 is speaking of a non-Christian say verse 14 is the key: "I am carnal, sold under sin." Then they point to verse 18, which says, "I know that in me (that is, in my flesh) dwelleth no good thing; for to will is present with me, but how to perform that which is good I find not." They conclude that has to be a non-Christian because a Christian knows how to do what's good. There seems to be an obvious lack of the Holy Spirit's power.

        (2) The peace of God

        The despair of verse 24—"Oh, wretched man that I am!"—seems far removed from the promise of Romans 5:1-2: "Being justified by faith, we have peace with God through our Lord Jesus Christ, by whom we have access by faith into this grace in which we stand, and rejoice in hope of the glory of God." The question may be asked, How can a man justified by faith be so wretched?

        (3) The freedom of believers

        Romans 6 has many examples of the believer's freedom from sin's power. Verse 2 says, "How shall we, that are dead to sin, live any longer in it?" Verses 6-7 say, "Our old man is crucified with [Christ], that the body of sin might be destroyed, that henceforth we should not serve sin. For he that is dead is freed from sin." Verses 11-12 say, "Reckon ye also yourselves to be dead indeed unto sin. . . . Let not sin, therefore, reign in your mortal body." Verse 17-18 say, "God be thanked, that whereas you were the servants of sin, ye have obeyed from the heart that form of doctrine which was delivered you. Being, then, made free from sin, ye became servants of righteousness." With all the evidence of chapter 6, the proponents of the non-Christian view ask how one who says, "I am carnal, sold under sin" (7:14), can be a Christian.

b) Stating its problems

The emphasis in chapter 6 is on the new creation, the new nature, the new identity, the new person in Christ, and the holiness of the believer. In his new redeemed self, the believer has broken sin's dominion. However, the emphasis of chapter 7 is different. Paul now gives the other side.

Every Christian knows that, even though he is a new creature in Christ, sin is still a problem. In fact, that conflict is pointed out in chapter 6: "Let not sin, therefore, reign in your mortal body, that ye should obey it in its lusts" (v. 12). In spite of all that Paul said in chapter 6 about the Christian's new nature, he never said the Christian wouldn't battle with sin. Verse 12 implies that we will. That implication is carried into verse 13: "Neither yield ye your members as instruments of unrighteousness unto sin." Because it is still possible for Christians to yield to sin, they are commanded not to.

In Romans 6:19 Paul says, "I speak after the manner of men because of the infirmity of your flesh; for as ye have yielded your members servants to uncleanness and to iniquity, unto iniquity; even so now yield your members servants to righteousness, unto holiness." The implication again is that a Christian could yield to sin.

So arguing that chapter 7 cannot refer to a Christian because of statements in chapter 6 is to misunderstand the intention of chapter 6.

2. The Christian view

a) The accurate description of a Christian

(1) Pursuing God

Paul says, "I delight in the law of God after the inward man" (Rom. 7:22). That certainly isn't something a non-Christian could accurately claim. Romans 8:7 says that the unregenerate person is not subject to the law of God.

In verse 25 Paul says, "I thank God through Jesus Christ, our Lord. So, then, with the mind I myself serve the law of God." That sounds like a Christian to me—thanking God through Jesus Christ our Lord and serving the law of God with the mind are the deepest longing of a Christian.

(2) Hating sin

Verse 15 describes Paul's thwarted desire to do what is right: "That which I do, I understand not; for what I would, that do I not; but what I hate, that do I." Does an unsaved person long to do what is right but inexplicably be prevented from doing it? Not according to Jeremiah, who said, "The heart is deceitful above all things, and desperately wicked" (Jer. 7:9).

Paul continues to explain the internal battle in verses 18-19, 21: "I know that in me (that is, in my flesh) dwelleth no good thing; for to will is present with me, but how to perform that which is good I find not. For the good that I would, I do not; but the evil which I would not, that I do. . . . I find then a law, that, when I would do good, evil is present with me." Something deep inside this person wants to do what is right. Nev-

151

ertheless an evil principle keeps that from being easily accomplished.

Romans 3 tells us that the unsaved person has no such longing to do the will of God. "There is none that understandeth, there is none that seeketh after God. . . . There is none that doeth good, no, not one. . . . There is no fear of God before their eyes" (vv. 11-12, 18). Paul says that an unbeliever does not pursue God's purposes or His holy law.

The conflict described in Romans 7 can be true of a redeemed person only. I don't believe an unsaved person experiences much of a battle at all. From God's perspective people are not good by nature but evil.

b) The acute debate over carnality

Another question has sparked an equally furious debate: What kind of Christian is Romans 7 talking about?

(1) The Christian of Romans 7 is spiritually immature

Some believe he's a carnal Christian—one with a low level of spirituality who is trying in his own strength to keep the law. One writer believes Romans 7 describes the "abject misery and failure of a Christian who attempts to please God under the Mosaic system" (Stanley D. Toussaint, "The Contrast Between the Spiritual Conflict in Romans 7 and Galatians 5," *Bibliotheca Sacra* 123 [Oct.-Dec. 1966]: 312).

(2) The Christian of Romans 7 is spiritually mature

Romans 7:14-25 describes a mature Christian, one who clearly sees the inability of his flesh to uphold the divine standard. The more spiritual a believer is, the greater his sensitivity to his shortcomings will be. An immature Christian doesn't have an honest self-perception. The legalist is under the illusion that he is spiritual. I believe Paul is describing himself in this chapter, which would seem obvious from his extensive use of the personal pronoun "I."

(a) Paul's confessions throughout Scripture

Some say Romans 7:14-25 describes Paul's struggle before he was saved or right after he was saved and was still spiritually immature. I disagree. I believe this passage describes Paul at the very height of his Christian perception, when he recognizes that he does not live up to the God's holy standards even though he desires to do so with all his heart. He finds himself debilitated by the ugly reality that sin is still present.

i) 1 Corinthians 15:9-10—Paul here said the same thing in other terms: "I am the least of the apostles, that am not fit to be called an apostle, because I persecuted the church of God. But by the grace of God I am what I am." Paul didn't feel fit to be an apostle because he had once persecuted the church.

ii) Ephesians 3:8—Paul considered himself as "less than the least of all saints." The fact that 1 Corinthians was written before Ephesians shows he became more humble as time went on. It appears that Paul saw himself as having fallen from the position of the least of the apostles to less than the least of all believers.

iii) 1 Timothy 1:12-16—Paul said, "I thank Christ Jesus, our Lord, who hath enabled me, in that he counted me faithful, putting me into the ministry, who was before a blasphemer, and a persecutor, and injurious; but I obtained mercy, because I did it ignorantly in unbelief. And the grace of our Lord was exceedingly abundant with faith and love which is in Christ Jesus.

153

This is a faithful saying, and worthy of all acceptance, that Christ Jesus came into the world to save sinners, of whom I am chief. Nevertheless, for this cause I obtained mercy." Paul wrote this after he wrote Ephesians. Having experienced more of God's mighty power, wisdom, and knowledge he became increasingly sensitive to the presence of sin in his life.

(*b*) Paul's emphasis through Romans 7

i) The terms he uses

The terms Paul uses in Romans 7 are so precise that we can't miss his struggle with sin. He states that he hates committing sin (v. 15), loves righteousness (vv. 19, 21), delights in the law of God from the bottom of his heart (v. 22), and thanks God for the deliverance that is his in Christ (v. 25). Those are the responses of a mature Christian.

ii) The transitions he makes

The change in verb tenses is a clue that this passage applies to a Christian. The verbs in Romans 7:7-13 are in the past tense. They refer to Paul's life before his conversion and the process of conviction he experienced when he stood face-to-face with the law of God. However, verses 14-25, where we see the battle with sin taking place, are in the present tense. That tells us Paul has moved out of the past—before he was redeemed—into the present.

Accompanying that change is a different relationship to sin. In Romans 7:11 Paul says, "Sin, taking occasion by the commandment, deceived me, and by it slew me." Sin killed Paul's hope and security in his self-righteousness. But in verses 14-25 we see Paul fighting with sin.

I believe Romans 7:14-25 is Paul's own testimony of life as a Spirit-controlled, mature believer. He loves the holy law of God with his whole heart but finds himself wrapped in human flesh and unable to fulfill it the way he wants to.

B. The Context of the Passage

Romans 7:14-25 continues Paul's discussion of the law. He previously was affirming that although nothing is wrong with the law, it can't save or sanctify on account of human weakness. Its chief value is in convicting us of sin. That's true both before and after we're saved, which is what Romans 7:14-25 illustrates. Sin does not obviate the law before we are saved, and it doesn't obviate it after we're saved, either. In fact, when you become a Christian, you should be more concerned about your sin than you were before you were saved. When the psalmist said, "Thy word have I hidden in mine heart, that I might not sin" (Psalm 119:11), he was saying that the Word of God in the heart leads to conviction. It isn't just information—it has power.

Lesson

Romans 7:14-25 is a picture of indwelling sin in the life of a believer. This passage is unique in that it contains a series of laments—desperate, repetitious cries of a distressed soul in great conflict. Each lament follows the same pattern. Paul first describes his condition, then gives proof of it, and then explains the source of the problem.

I. THE STRUGGLE RECORDED (vv. 14-23)

A. The First Lament (vv. 14-17)

1. The condition of carnality (v. 14)

"For we know that the law is spiritual: but I am carnal, sold under sin."

155

a) The affirmation of spirituality

The word *for* tells us that Paul is not introducing a new subject; he's continuing the same subject from the prior passage about the law's revealing our sin. Paul continues to answer the hypothetical accusation that his preaching of salvation by grace through faith apart from the law implies that the law is evil. He states to the contrary that "the law is spiritual," meaning that it comes from the Spirit of God, reflecting His holy, just, and good nature (cf. v. 12).

b) The admission of sinfulness

(1) The barrier to obedience

Although Paul delights in God's law, he confesses there is a barrier that prevents him from obeying it: his carnal or fleshly nature. He doesn't say he was in the flesh or controlled by the flesh. Romans 7:5 makes clear that Christians cannot be considered as being in the flesh: "When we were in the flesh, the sinful impulses, which were by the law, did work in our members to bring forth fruit unto death." Romans 8:8-9 says to its Christian audience, "They that are in the flesh cannot please God. But ye are not in the flesh." The phrase "in the flesh" refers to an unregenerate condition.

Although Christians are not in the flesh, the flesh is still in us. We're no longer held captive to it, but we can still act fleshly, or carnally. In 1 Corinthians 3 Paul says, "I, brethren, could not speak unto you as unto spiritual, but as unto carnal, even as unto babes in Christ. . . . For ye are yet carnal; for whereas there is among you envying, and strife, and divisions, are ye not carnal, and walk as men?" (vv. 1, 3). He reproved the Corinthian Christians for acting as if they were in the flesh.

In Romans 7 Paul says, "I know that in me (that is, in my flesh) dwelleth no good thing. . . . With

156

the mind I myself serve the law of God; but with the flesh, the law of sin" (vv. 18, 25). He admits that the flesh is still present. *Flesh* is simply a term for our humanness.

When Paul said, "Let not sin, therefore, reign in your mortal body" (Rom. 6:12), he implied that it doesn't reign in the believer's renewed mind, although it still affects it. When he dies, he immediately goes to heaven, because the flesh is the only thing that keeps the believer from being fit for heaven.

Any Christian could make the statement in verse 14. Saying you're carnal is the same as saying you're a sinner. For example, when I am angry, insensitive, or don't pursue God as diligently as I desire, I see my humanness getting in the way of accomplishing all I ought to do.

(2) The bondage to sin

(a) The explanation

Paul states in verse 14 that he is "sold under sin." Verse 23 gives us a similar statement: "I see another law in my members, warring against the law of my mind, and bringing me into captivity to the law of sin." But how can that be since Christians have been delivered from sin? The phrase "sold under sin" is literally "having been sold under *the* sin" in the Greek text. That puts emphasis on the sin principle, the product of the Fall of man, which continues to reside in the believer's body, not the individual deeds committed.

Being "sold under sin" doesn't mean Paul actively committed himself to sinning, as is said about Ahab in 1 Kings 21:20, 25 and of the idolatrous Israelites in 2 Kings 17:17. Paul recognized that in this life believers will constantly have to battle sin on account of their human flesh. Every time you sin, you lose the battle and become, in a sense, captive to sin.

Our incorruptible nature isn't in view in verse 14; the physical, human nature is. The law, or principle, of sin resides in our bodily "members" (v. 23), which include the physical, emotional, intellectual, and volitional parts of man.

Can Paul's lament of being sold under sin come from a true believer? In Psalm 51:5 David says, "Surely I have been a sinner from birth, sinful from the time my mother conceived me" (NIV*). That may sound like a man who has never been redeemed, but David was simply looking at one reality about himself. His lament is similar to that of Isaiah, who upon seeing a vision of God said, "Woe is me! For I am undone, because I am a man of unclean lips, and I dwell in the midst of a people of unclean lips" (Isa. 6:5). All the prophet could see against the glorious holiness of God was his own sin.

(b) The evidence

Paul's lament is evidence of the apostle's maturity. He knew that the law is spiritual, holy, just, and good but that he remained fleshly. He reiterates that perception in 1 Timothy 1:15, where he admits to being the chief of sinners. That is a legitimate and desirable perception for a Christian to have. Not only can a Christian say that he is in bondage to sin, though redeemed, but the more spiritual he is, the more likely he is to say this. It is a perception of any mature Christian; not of one who has a poor self-image.

Paul puts all our experiences with sin into words in Romans 7:14-25. We all know there's

*New International Version.

sin in our lives even though it shouldn't be there. Although sin is not the product of our new self, we're still bound to some degree by the body we dwell in. Verse 14 could be paraphrased, "The law is spiritual, but I am unspiritual, experiencing a bondage to sin at times."

Commentator C. E. B. Cranfield wrote, "The more seriously a Christian strives to live from grace and to submit to the discipline of the gospel, the more sensitive he becomes to . . . the fact that even his very best acts and activities are disfigured by the egotism which is still powerful within him—and no less evil because it is often more subtly disguised than formerly" (*A Critical and Exegetical Commentary on the Epistle to the Romans*, vol. 1 [Edinburgh: T & T Clark, 1975], p. 358). He's right. That sinful presence of the flesh is still there. Sin is so wretched that, even when a person has been redeemed, it still hangs on to some degree.

2. The proof of the problem (v. 15)

"That which I do I understand [or, know] not; for what I would, that do I not; but what I hate, that do I."

A self-righteous person deceives himself into thinking he is moral, but a Christian led by the Spirit will not. He sees the proof in him of indwelling sin. The word translated "understand" or "know" implies an intimate love (e.g., Gen. 4:1). To make his point, not only does Paul say that he does not love what he ends up doing but also that he hates doing it. His failure to do what he desired and his practice of doing what he hated reflects a profound inner turmoil. His will was frustrated by his sinful flesh. It's not that evil won all the time, but that he was frustrated in his attempt to perfectly obey God's entire law.

If you're a Christian, you can identify with that frustration. For instance, no sooner are you complimented for

having done something right then you become proud—
and now you've just done something wrong. The road
to spirituality is paved with a sense of your own wretchedness, not your own self-glory. The spiritual man has a
broken and contrite heart, realizing he can't be all that
God wants him to be. Sad to say, many Christians have
yet to reach this point. That's not because they're so
holy; it's because their comprehension of God's holy
law is so shallow.

3. The source of the struggle (vv. 16-17)

"If, then, I do that which I would not, I consent unto the
law that it is good. Now, then, it is no more I that do it,
but sin that dwelleth in me."

Do you know what makes a Christian want to carry out
God's law? His new nature within, which according to 1
John 3:9 does not sin. When he goes against his new nature, it isn't the law that is responsible but the sin that
still resides in his frail human body. A Christian will
naturally pursue the moral excellence of God's law. The
more mature a Christian is—the more he loves the Lord,
submits to the Spirit's direction in his life, and grows in
his understanding of God's holiness—the greater will be
his longing to fulfill the law.

Was Paul Shirking His Responsibility?

Verse 17 sounds like Paul refuses to take the blame for his sin. It's
as if he's blaming an inanimate object instead of himself. However,
in verse 14 Paul acknowledges that he is sinful. We can all identify
with his desire to live for God as well as with his failure to be as
holy as He wants us to be. Accepting responsibility for our failure
challenges the philosophical dualism teaching that God doesn't
hold us responsible for our sin because sin is tied to our old nature.
That view concludes we should go ahead and sin because we can't
do anything about our tendency to sin. But we must reject that
kind of thinking. Although a Christian will sin less and less as he
matures, he at the same time will be more aware of the sin in his
life because of his increased understanding of God's law.

Verse 17 goes beyond Paul's admitting that he is responsible for sin. He specifies what part of him is responsible by making a more technical distinction: the sin that dwells in his flesh. Verse 17 says, "Now, then, it is no more I . . . but sin." The Greek phrase *de ouketi* ("now . . . no more"; a negative adverb of time) means from this point on something has changed. An unbeliever could never claim a new beginning that marks a permanent change from the past. Whatever he was, he still is. But when Christ comes into a believer's life and gives him a new spiritual nature, the believer can accurately claim that he is no longer the same.

Paul's reasoning in verse 17 is reminiscent of Galatians 2:20: "I [the old nature] am crucified with Christ: nevertheless I live, yet not I, but Christ liveth in me; and the life which I now live in the flesh I live by the faith of the Son of God, who loved me and gave himself for me." After salvation, sin no longer resides in man's innermost self, which is recreated to be like Christ. Yet it finds its residual dwelling in our flesh. That's why Paul said nothing good dwelt in his flesh (v. 18).

Conclusion

A. The Failure of the Flesh

There's a big difference between surviving sin and reigning sin: sin no longer reigns in us, but it does survive in us. We are like an artistically unskilled person who has a beautiful picture in clear view but has no ability to actually paint it. He's debilitated by his physical incapacity. The fault is not with the scene but with his inability. That's where the Christian finds his frustration. The problem is not the law; it is our inability to keep the law because of our sinful flesh. That is why we must ask the Master Artist to put His hand on ours to help us paint the strokes we could have never painted independently of Him. We can experience victory over sin only when we yield ourselves to the One who can overcome the flesh.

B. The Solution of the Spirit

Galatians 5:17 says, "The flesh lusteth against the Spirit, and the Spirit against the flesh; and these are contrary the one to the other, so that ye cannot do the things that ye would." Romans 7 echoes that battle. Galatians 5:16 tells us how to win: "This I say then, walk in the Spirit, and ye shall not fulfill the lust of the flesh." The Holy Spirit gives us victory. But let me warn you that the more victory you experience as you mature in Christ, the more you will recognize sin in your life. The Spirit of God is the resource for those whose deepest longing is to fulfill the law of God but are distressed because they fail to obey it perfectly. Praise God that we will one day leave our sinful flesh behind to enter glory and perfectly fulfill His law.

Focusing on the Facts

1. Identify the conflict raging within Paul in Romans 7:14-25 (see p. 148).
2. What has been the major debate regarding that passage (see p. 148)?
3. Why do some conclude that Paul was referring to himself before he came to Christ (see pp. 149-50)?
4. When does sin's dominion over a person come to an end? What implications in Romans 6 support your answer (see p. 150)?
5. What desire of Paul shows that he is speaking from a Christian perspective (see p. 151)?
6. What does Romans 3:11-12, 18 tell us about an unbeliever's regard for God (see p. 152)?
7. Explain the debate about the maturity of the Christian in view in Romans 7:14-25 (see p. 152).
8. The more _____ a believer is, the greater his _____ to his shortcomings will be (see p. 152).
9. Chart Paul's evaluation of himself in 1 Corinthians 15:9-10, Ephesians 3:8, and 1 Timothy 1:12-16 (see pp. 153-54).
10. What transitions take place in Romans 7 leading us to conclude that verses 14-25 are the testimony of a mature believer (see pp. 154-55)?
11. Although Paul wanted to obey God's law, what barrier prevented him from obeying it fully (see p. 156)?

162

12. Where does sin reign, according to Romans 6:12 (see p. 157)?
13. What did Paul mean when he said he was "sold under sin" (Rom. 7:14; see pp. 157-58)?
14. Is it a sign of maturity to admit one's bondage to sin? Explain (see p. 158).
15. Describe the profound inner turmoil Paul experienced (Rom. 7:15; see p. 159).
16. The road to spirituality is paved with a sense of your own _____, not your own _____ (see p. 160).
17. Why do many Christians not have broken and contrite hearts over their sin (see p. 160)?
18. What part of a Christian makes him want to carry out God's law? Explain the relationship between his longing to fulfill that law and spiritual maturity (see p. 160).
19. Why could an unbeliever never claim a new beginning marking a permanent change from the past (see p. 161)?
20. What is the only way believers can experience victory over sin? Explain (see pp. 161-62).

Pondering the Principles

1. If you're a Christian, the conflict of delighting in God's will but failing to carry it out perfectly should be present in your life. However, knowing that it is normal for Christians to sin once in a while, don't succumb to the temptation of rationalizing your sin. Sin brings nothing but guilt, misery, and despair to the person who refuses to deal with it as it appears in his life. Follow the lead of the psalmist who said, "Thy word have I hidden in mine heart, that I might not sin against thee" (Ps. 119:11).

2. Memorize Galatians 5:16: "Walk by the Spirit, and you will not carry out the desire of the flesh." We can win the battle over the sinful desires of our flesh when we walk by the Spirit, a step-by-step process of depending on His guidance to avoid and resist temptation. Are you communing daily with God in prayer? When you encounter temptations, is your first reaction to seek the Spirit's wisdom on how to have victory? Take time now to praise God for the resource we have in the Spirit and the promise we have in one day being totally free from sin.

9
The Believer and Indwelling Sin—Part 2

Outline

Introduction
A. Our Sensitivity to Sin
B. The Consequences of Sin

Review
I. The Struggle Recorded (vv. 14-23)
   A. The First Lament (vv. 14-17)
      1. The condition of carnality (v. 14)
      2. The proof of the problem (v. 15)
      3. The source of the struggle (vv. 16-17)

Lesson
   B. The Second Lament (vv. 18-20)
      1. The condition of carnality (v. 18a)
      2. The proof of the problem (vv. 18b-19)
      3. The source of the struggle (v. 20)
   C. The Third Lament (vv. 21-23)
      1. The condition of carnality (v. 21)
      2. The proof of the problem (vv. 22-23a)
        a) The inward delight (v. 22)
        b) The outward discord (v. 23a)
      3. The source of the struggle (v. 23b)
II. The Solution Revealed (vv. 24-25)
   A. The Self-Evaluation of a Sinner (v. 24a)
      1. Explained
      2. Exemplified
        a) Psalm 6
        b) Psalm 38
        c) Psalm 130

B. The Deliverance from Death (vv. 24*b*-25*a*)
   1. The appeal for help (v. 24*b*)
   2. The assurance of hope (v. 25*a*)
      a) Romans 8
      b) 1 Corinthians 15
      c) 2 Corinthians 5
      d) Philippians 3:20-21
C. The Continuation of the Conflict (v. 25*b*)

Introduction

A. Our Sensitivity to Sin

A young man mockingly said to a preacher, "You say that unsaved people carry a great weight of sin. Frankly, I feel nothing. How heavy is sin? Ten pounds? Fifty pounds? Eighty pounds? A hundred pounds?" The preacher thought for a moment and gently replied, "If you laid a four-hundred-pound weight on a corpse, would it feel the load?" The young man said, "Of course not: it's dead." The preacher replied, "The person who doesn't know Christ is equally dead. And though the load is great, he feels none of it."

The believer is not indifferent to the weight of sin as the unbeliever is. He is actually hypersensitive to sin. Having come to Jesus Christ, his senses are awakened to the reality of sin. His sensitivity to sin intensifies as he matures spiritually. Such sensitivity prompted a saint as great as Chrysostom, the fourth-century church Father, to say he feared nothing but sin (*Second Homily on Eutropius*).

When confronted with the message of salvation by grace, an unbeliever retorted, "If I believed your doctrine that salvation is only a matter of faith, and was sure I could be so easily converted, I would believe and then take my fill of sin." Clearly he did not understand that a true Christian could never tolerate the kind of sinful indulgence he had in mind.

Coming to faith in Christ brings an overwhelming sense of sin. A Christian feels the true weight of sin while an unbeliever does not. Ephesians 2:1 says unbelievers are "dead in trespasses and sins." But a Christian under grace hates the evil that is in him. He does not seek not to fill up his life with sin but to empty it.

B. The Consequences of Sin

As Christians, we should be aware of the serious consequences of sin:

1. The Holy Spirit is grieved (Eph. 4:30).

2. Our prayers go unanswered (1 Pet. 3:7).

3. Our life becomes powerless (1 Cor. 9:27). Paul feared the power of sin would disqualify himself from the ministry.

4. Our praise is unacceptable (Ps. 33:1). The psalmist said, "Praise is fitting to the upright." Conversely, praise is not fitting for those who are not.

5. God's blessing is withheld (Jer. 5:25). Jeremiah rebuked the nation of Israel, saying, "Your sins have withheld good things from you."

6. Our joy is forfeited (Ps. 51:12). When confronted with his sin, David asked God to restore to him the joy of His salvation.

7. God's chastening is administered (Heb. 12:5-11).

8. Our spiritual growth is hindered (1 Cor. 3:1-3). The apostle Paul couldn't offer the Corinthians the spiritual nourishment he wanted them to experience because they were so sinful.

9. Our service is limited (2 Tim. 2:21). Paul said we must have pure lives to be vessels fit for the Master's use.

10. Our fellowship is polluted (1 Cor. 10:21). Paul instructs us in 1 Corinthians 11:28-29 to cleanse own hearts before God before we come to the Lord's Table.

11. Our lives are endangered (1 Cor. 11:30; 1 John 5:16).

12. God is dishonored (1 Cor. 6:19-20). Because our bodies are the temple of the Lord, we dishonor Him when we bring them into contact with sin.

None of us wants to do any of those things. On the contrary, we can more readily identify with the psalmist who said, "As the hart [deer] panteth after the water brooks, so panteth my soul after thee, O God" (Ps. 42:1).

When an individual comes to faith in Jesus Christ, God plants a new nature within him that longs for the things of God and despises sin. That is the testimony of the apostle Paul in Romans 7:14-25—a man in conflict who hated sin and yearned to obey the law of God. Such conflict is not experienced by unredeemed men, who according to John 3:19-20 love darkness and hate righteousness. Reflecting on the Word of God, the psalmist said, "Through thy precepts I get understanding; therefore, I hate every false way" (Ps. 119:104).

Puritan Thomas Watson said that a sign of sanctification is a hatred for sin. A hypocrite may leave sin yet love it—as a snake sheds its skin but keeps its venom—but a sanctified person not only leaves sin, but he loathes it. God has changed our nature: He has put on us the breastplate of holiness, which, though it may be shot at, can never be shot through (*A Body of Divinity* [London: Banner of Truth, 1970], pp. 246, 250).

Review

I. THE STRUGGLE RECORDED (vv. 14-23)

A. The First Lament (vv. 14-17; see pp. 155-61)

1. The condition of carnality (v. 14; see pp. 155-59)

Paul found himself still being victimized by sin even though he was redeemed.

2. The proof of the problem (v. 15; see pp. 159-60)

Paul was experiencing conflict between desiring to obey God's law and being frustrated in not being able to live up to that standard all the time. It's a sign of immaturity to believe you've arrived at a point of spiritual perfection. The apostle Paul admitted he hadn't obtained that goal, nevertheless he continued to press toward it (Phil. 3:12-14). That's the humility that comes from right spiritual perception. If we understand God's law we're going to see ourselves as falling short.

3. The source of the struggle (vv. 16-17; pp. 160-61)

The source of Paul's problem was the sin that continued to dwell in his human nature. It conflicted with his new nature in Christ received at salvation. Even though we're redeemed, sin prevents us from consistently fulfilling our desire to obey God's law.

I believe every child of God who is walking in obedience to God laments the reality of his sin. In 1 John 1:8-10 we see we're to acknowledge and confess our sin, and in Psalm 97:10 we see we're to love the Lord while hating evil.

Lesson

B. The Second Lament (vv. 18-20)

1. The condition of carnality (v. 18a)

"I know that in me (that is, in my flesh) dwelleth no good thing."

Paul gave a more technical identification of the part of him that was actually sinning than he had previously. He wanted to emphasize that it wasn't his new incorruptible nature that was failing to obey God's law; it was the sin that dwelled in his flesh. Paul admitted that there was nothing good in his unredeemed humanity.

The flesh, however, isn't necessarily evil in and of itself, but it's where sin finds its base of operation.

2. The proof of the problem (vv. 18*b*-19)

"To will is present with me, but how to perform that which is good I find not. For the good that I would, I do not; but the evil which I would not, that I do."

Paul did not say he couldn't figure out how to do anything right. He said he can't do it to the extent his heart longed to. If you look at your spiritual growth as a Christian, you should be able to recognize a greater hatred for sin now than you did before you understood how serious sin is and how holy God is. Although spiritual growth results in a decreasing frequency of sin, it inversely involves a heightened sensitivity to it.

You probably will not find any writer in the Old Testament who was more sensitive to his sin than David, the king through whom the Messiah came (Matt. 21:9, 15) and a man after God's own heart (1 Sam. 13:14). In his psalms David cried out to God for mercy in the midst of his sinfulness (e.g., Ps. 32; 51). David's close relationship with the Lord caused him to have a broken heart when he sinned (Ps. 51:17). That kind of struggle with sin is characteristic of a regenerate man.

3. The source of the struggle (v. 20)

"If I do that I would not, it is no more I that do it, but sin that dwelleth in me."

Although Paul had a new nature, he still fought against sin—and often lost. Those losses seemed overwhelming to him against the perfection of God's holy law. Nevertheless, his sensitivity to sin was a normal result of justification by faith.

You might expect Paul to stop at this point, having adequately made his point. But he starts a third lament to emphasize his frustration and sorrow over sin.

C. The Third Lament (vv. 21-23)

1. The condition of carnality (v. 21)

"I find then a law, that, when I would do good, evil is present with me."

Paul again lamented the condition of indwelling sin. He used the Greek word translated "law" as a literary device to refer to a principle. In contrast to the law of God, he saw another law or standard that was making demands on him: the principle of evil. The Greek text literally says that evil lies close at hand. Evil battles every good thought, word, and deed. Rather than our sin nature's being eradicated in this life, as some theologians have concluded, Paul tells us that evil is present within us, creating conflict.

2. The proof of the problem (vv. 22-23a)

a) The inward delight (v. 22)

"For I delight in the law of God after the inward man."

In his new spiritual nature, Paul delighted in God's law. Psalm 119 is an Old Testament parallel to Romans 7. In verse 77 the psalmist writes, "Let thy tender mercies come unto me, that I may live; for thy law is my delight." Paul might well have had that psalm in mind when he wrote Romans 7. Psalm 119:111 says, "Thy testimonies have I taken as an heritage forever; for they are the rejoicing of my heart." Verse 20 says, "My soul breaketh for the longing that it has unto thine ordinances at all times."

Likewise, the mark of the truly spiritual man in Psalm 1:2 is that "his delight is in the law of the Lord; and in his law doth he meditate day and night." The regenerate man is marked by a love for the Word of God.

171

The phrase "after the inward man" could be translated "from the bottom of my heart." Paul had a great love for the law of God. That redeemed inward part of man "is renewed day by day" (2 Cor. 4:16) and is "strengthened with might by [God's] Spirit" (Eph. 3:16). The truest expression of a redeemed believer is to delight in God's law.

   b) The outward discord (v. 23*a*)

"But I see another law in my members, warring against the law of my mind."

The channels through which this sin principle is expressed are the "members," the parts of the body that are subject to our unredeemed humanness. This law isn't in Paul's inner man; it's in his outer man.

Paul equated the law of God with the law of his mind, because the deepest desire of his inner man was to obey the law of God. If he were an unbeliever, the law of his mind would be just as rotten as the law of his members, for "the carnal mind is enmity against God" (Rom. 8:7).

3. The source of the struggle (v. 23*b*)

"Bringing me into captivity to the law of sin which is in my members."

Paul identified the source of his problems as the sin that resided in him. Sometimes the battle was won by the law of his members, which brought him into captivity. That implied Paul was speaking as a redeemed person, because unredeemed people can't be brought into captivity—they're already there. When sin wins the victory in the spiritual struggle, the believer becomes a slave to the sin that, at least temporarily, masters him.

The Irony of Victory and Defeat

The author of Psalm 119 experienced the same conflict as Paul. His psalm reflects his deep longing for the things of God.

1. Verses 81-83—"My soul fainteth for thy salvation, but I hope in thy word. Mine eyes fail for thy word, saying, When wilt thou comfort me? For I am become like a wineskin in the smoke; yet do I not forget thy statutes."

2. Verse 92—"Unless thy law had been my delight, I should then have perished in mine affliction."

3. Verse 97—"Oh, how I love thy law! It is my meditation all the day."

4. Verse 113—"I hate vain thoughts, but thy law do I love."

5. Verse 131—"I opened my mouth, and panted; for I longed for thy commandments."

6. Verse 143—"Trouble and anguish have taken hold of me; yet thy commandments are my delight."

7. Verse 163—"I hate and abhor lying, but thy law do I love."

8. Verse 165—"Great peace have they who love thy law, and nothing shall offend them."

9. Verse 174—"I have longed for thy salvation, O Lord, and thy law is my delight."

The measure of spirituality that the psalmist expresses is somewhat intimidating. That is why the last verse in Psalm 119 is so surprising: "I have gone astray like a lost sheep. Seek thy servant; for I do not forget thy commandments" (v. 176). You might think that a person with such an intense love for God's law would not experience the failure of going astray spiritually. But that is the conflict all believers experience.

Why do we sin? Because God didn't do a good enough job when He saved us? Because He gave us a new nature that isn't complete? Because we're not prepared for heaven, and we still need to earn our way? No. It's because sin is still present in our humanness, which includes the mind, emotions, and body.

In 2 Corinthians 10:3 Paul says, "Though we walk in the flesh, we do not war after the flesh (for the weapons of our warfare are not carnal, but mighty through God to the pulling down of strongholds)." Although we are still have physical bodies, we are engaged in spiritual warfare using spiritual resources.

Paul's three laments reveal a condition of conflict in the life of every believer. They give evidence of that conflict by admitting the inability of a believer to do God's will to the extent he ought to. They identify the source of the conflict—indwelling sin. From that conflict the believer cries out for deliverance.

II. THE SOLUTION REVEALED (vv. 24-25)

A. The Self-Evaluation of a Sinner (v. 24a)

"Oh, wretched man that I am."

1. Explained

As if three laments aren't enough, Paul lets out a cry in verse 24 that exceeds them in intensity. He cries out in the distress and the frustration of his spiritual conflict. Can this be the despair of a Christian, let alone that of the apostle Paul? Commentator Robert Haldane once said that men perceive themselves to be sinners in proportion to what they perceive about the holiness of God and His law.

2. Exemplified

a) Psalm 6—David cried out, "O Lord, rebuke me not in thine anger, neither chasten me in thy hot displeasure. Have mercy upon me, O Lord; for I am weak. O Lord, heal me; for my bones are vexed. My soul is also very vexed [terrified]; but thou, O Lord, how long? Return, O Lord, deliver my soul: oh, save me for thy mercies' sake. For in death there is no remembrance of thee; in sheol who shall give thee thanks? I am weary with my groaning; all the night make I my bed to swim; I water my couch with my tears" (vv. 1-6). David was saying, "I'm so sick and tired of not being everything I ought to be!"

b) Psalm 38—Similarly, David said, "O Lord, rebuke me not in thy wrath; neither chasten me in thy hot displeasure. For thine arrows stick fast in me, and thy hand presseth me greatly. There is no soundness in my flesh because of thine anger; neither is there any rest in my bones because of my sin. For mine iniquities are gone over mine head; like an heavy burden they are too heavy for me. My wounds are repulsive and corrupt because of my foolishness. I am troubled; I am bowed down greatly; I go mourning all the day long. For my loins are filled with a loathsome disease, and there is no soundness in my flesh. I am feeble and very broken; I have roared by reason of the disquietness of my heart. Lord, all my desire is before thee" (vv. 1-9). If David's desire was before the Lord, how could he get into such a mess? That's the battle that the believer faces. Like Paul, David wanted to be more than he was, and he found himself debilitated by his humanness.

c) Psalm 130—The psalmist wrote, "Out of the depths have I cried unto thee, O Lord. Lord, hear my voice; let thine ears be attentive to the voice of my supplications. If thou, Lord, shouldest mark iniquities, O Lord, who shall stand? But there is forgiveness with thee, that thou mayest be feared. I wait for the Lord, my soul doth wait, and in his word do I hope" (vv. 1-5). There again we see the despair of a godly person over sin.

B. The Deliverance from Death (vv. 24*b*-25*a*)

1. The appeal for help (v. 24*b*)

"Who shall deliver me from the body of this death?"

Paul rhetorically asks who will rescue him from the sin that resides in his body. The Greek word translated "deliver" was used to describe a soldier who ran to his comrade in the midst of a battle to rescue him from the enemy. "The body of this death" literally refers to our physical body that is subject to sin and death.

175

I read that near Tarsus, where Paul was born, lived a tribe that that inflicted a gruesome penalty upon murderers. They fastened the body of the victim to that of the killer, tying shoulder to shoulder, back to back, arm to arm, and then drove the murderer from the community. The bonds were so tight that the murderer could not free himself, and after a few days the decay in the body transferred itself to his living flesh. Paul might have had that gruesome punishment in mind in expressing here his desire to be rid of the sin that clung to his flesh.

2. The assurance of hope (v. 25*a*)

"I thank God through Jesus Christ, our Lord."

a) Romans 8—Paul gratefully expresses assurance of triumph through Jesus Christ over the conflict with sin. I believe that's what Paul had in mind when he said, "I reckon that the sufferings of this present time are not worthy to be compared with the glory which shall be revealed in us. For the earnest expectation of the creation waiteth for the manifestation of the sons of God. . . . The whole creation groaneth and travaileth in pain together until now. And not only they, but ourselves also, who have the first fruits of the Spirit, even we ourselves groan within ourselves, waiting for the adoption, that is, the redemption of our body" (Rom. 8:18-19, 22-23). Christians await the final phase of salvation. We're still looking to that day when we are redeemed in the body as well as soul. So Paul thanks God in Romans 7:25 that the end of the conflict will come through Christ when we enter into His presence and are glorified.

b) 1 Corinthians 15—Paul said, "This corruptible must put on incorruption, and this mortal must put on immortality. . . . Thanks be to God, who giveth us the victory through our Lord Jesus Christ" (vv. 53, 57). That is almost the same phrase he uses in Romans 7:25 in reference to our bodily resurrection and glorification.

c) 2 Corinthians 5—Paul said, "We that are in this tabernacle [body] do groan, being burdened [with our humanness]; not that we would be unclothed, but clothed upon, that mortality might be swallowed up of life" (v. 4).

d) Philippians 3:20-21—Paul said, "We look for the Savior, the Lord Jesus Christ, who shall change our lowly body, that it may be fashioned like his glorious body." Ours is a triumphant hope!

C. The Continuation of the Conflict (v. 25b)

"So, then, with the mind I myself serve the law of God; but with the flesh, the law of sin."

Until the day we are glorified, the battle goes on. Tennyson wrote, "Ah for a new man to arise in me, that the man I am may cease to be!" (*Maud,* x.5). The battle won't be over until Jesus gives us immortality. Full deliverance awaits glorification. But that's not to say we can't experience victory here and now in the power of the Holy Spirit.

Focusing on the Facts

1. Rather than being indifferent to the weight of sin, the believer is actually _____ to it (see p. 166).
2. List five consequences of sin (see pp. 167-68).
3. Explain the sign of sanctification mentioned by Thomas Watson (see p. 168).
4. What does the apostle Paul admit he has not yet attained in Philippians 3:12-14 (see p. 169)?
5. Although spiritual growth results in a _____ frequency of sin, it inversely involves a _____ sensitivity to it (see p. 170).
6. What law—in addition to God's law—was making demands on Paul (see p. 171)?
7. What are the channels through which the sin principle is expressed in believers (see p. 172)?
8. How does Paul's being brought into captivity imply that he is a believer (see p. 172)?
9. Like Paul, what did the writer of Psalm 119 delight in? What is surprising in light of his spiritual maturity (Ps. 119:176; see pp. 172-73)?

10. Men perceive themselves to be _____ in proportion as they have previously discovered the _____ of God and His law (see p. 174).

11. What was Paul's assurance of hope for victory over sin? Support your answer with Scripture (see pp. 176-77).

12. What does full deliverance from sin await (see p. 177)?

Pondering the Principles

1. Study the list of consequences of sinning on pages 167-68. Look up the Scripture references listed and be familiar with them so that you will be less apt to fall before temptation to sin next time.

2. Read Psalm 119. Let the psalmist serve as a model to you to help strengthen your love for God's Word.

3. Give thanks to God that you are a new creation in Christ. Confess to Him that although you love His law and long to do what's right, there's something in you that wars against that desire. Next, ask that He would give you victory until Jesus gives you a body fashioned like His own. Memorize 1 John 3:2-3: "Beloved, now we are children of God, and it has not appeared as yet what we shall be. We know that, when He appears, we shall be like Him, because we shall see Him just as He is. And everyone who has this hope fixed on Him purifies himself, just as He is pure" (NASB). Is your hope fixed on your glorification when Christ returns? Is that hope having a purifying effect on your life-style in the meantime?

Scripture Index

Topical Index

flesh, 110-12. *See also* Sin, body of

law, 113. *See also* Law of God

sin, 112. *See also* Sin

transgression of, 8

Marriage

adultery, 105

bigamy, 105

divorce, 105

legal duration of, 104-6

remarriage, 105

Maturity, spiritual. *See* Sanctification

McCheyne, Robert Murray, "Jehovah Tsidkenu," 141-42

Mormonism, 54

Moule, Bishop Handley, 23-24, 32

Murray, John, 32, 135

Nature of believer. *See* Sanctification

Needham, David C., 42, 52

Newton, John, transformation of, 28-29, 42

Obedience. *See* Sanctification

O'Conner, Richard, 84

Old life vs. new life. *See* Sanctification

Old man vs. new man. *See* Sanctification

Old nature vs. new nature. *See* Sanctification

Oswald, Lee Harvey, 104

Paul

spiritual conviction of apostle, 128-39

spiritual struggle of apostle, 147-77

transformation of apostle, 29

Perfectionism, doctrine of, refuted, 16-17, 34-35, 38, 41, 52, 85, 150

Position vs. practice in Christ. *See* Sanctification

Psychology, reforming behavior and, 130-31

Rasputin, 10

Reforming behavior. *See* Psychology

Religion. *See* Legalism

Remarriage. *See* Marriage

Repentance. *See* Law of God, purpose of; Salvation

Resolutions. *See* Psychology

Responsibility. *See* Blame

Righteousness. *See* Sanctification

Romanovs, 10

Romans, outline of book of, 8, 65, 121-22

Salvation

baptism and. *See* Baptism

determining, 136

forensic view of, 17-18

by grace. *See* Justification

justification. *See* Justification

nonexperiential nature of, 51

security of, 10

source of, 71, 107

by works. *See* Legalism

Sanctification, 8-9, 11, 65

believers' baptism into Christ, 17-21, 51

believers' death and resurrection with Christ, 21-24, 40-41, 50-51, 71, 106-7

believers' death to sin, 39-42, 52-54

believers' freedom from sin, 30-39, 43, 51, 65, 92

triumph over. *See*
  Sanctification
See also Man
Spirituality. *See* Sanctification
Struggle, spiritual. *See*
  Sanctification
Suicide, Christians and, 51

Temptation
  and body. *See* Sin, body of
  triumph over, 53
  and world, 39, 55
  See also Sanctification, spiritual struggle
Tennyson, Lord Alfred, 177
Testimony, sense of shame in a
  Christian's, 87-88

Theosophy, 54
Toplady, Augustus, 42
Toussaint, Stanley D., 152
Transformation of believer. *See*
  Sanctification
Trials. *See* Sanctification, spiritual struggle

Victory. *See* Glorification,
  Sanctification

Watson, Thomas, 168
Watts, Isaac, 53
Wesley, Charles, 24
Wilde, Oscar, 84

Moody Press, a ministry of the Moody Bible Institute, is designed for education, evangelization, and edification. If we may assist you in knowing more about Christ and the Christian life, please write us without obligation: Moody Press, c/o MLM, Chicago, Illinois 60610.